Contents

I would like to thank everyone who humoured
a pen-wielding, middle-aged writer by answering
his questions, as well as family and friends who
encouraged him to write this book. In addition, I am very
grateful to Ian McCullough for his terrific cover –
I hope the book lives up to it!

On an Offa Bus

Encounters and thoughts on a border land

Gareth Wheatley

On an Offa Bus
First published in Wales in 2009
by
BRIDGE BOOKS
61 Park Avenue
WREXHAM
LL12 7AW

© 2009 text and illustrations Gareth Wheatley
© 2009 typesetting and design Bridge Books

A CIP entry for this book is available from the British Library

ISBN 978-1-84494-061-5

Printed and bound
by
Gutenberg Press Ltd
Malta

The Author

GARETH WHEATLEY WAS BORN and brought up in Gower, near Swansea, before emigrating to Australia as a little boy. As dusk began to make its presence felt at the end of that first exciting day, an old Aussie had told the little boy and his family all about the poisonous plants and slavering animals waiting to do them serious harm if they dared set foot outside the house. The little boy had asked a question, 'But isn't the toilet down the end of the garden?' The old Aussie had smiled. 'Yes. Good luck!'

Somehow surviving the night, the little boy became a teenager and enjoyed the Australian way of life before returning to Britain and arriving back in Swansea with his parents and sister in the middle of what he remembers as a dank, late November day. Within a few weeks of leaving a mixed Sydney high school, which might have been transplanted from California, he was wandering around a British all -boys grammar school where masters wore gowns and some even tried to teach him Latin. It is little wonder the teenager tried to escape to a fantasy land through writing down dark thoughts on dark Welsh winter evenings. He is still writing today – film scripts, a dodgy novel and now *On an Offa Bus*, which he hopes will show that his thoughts are lighter than they used to be!

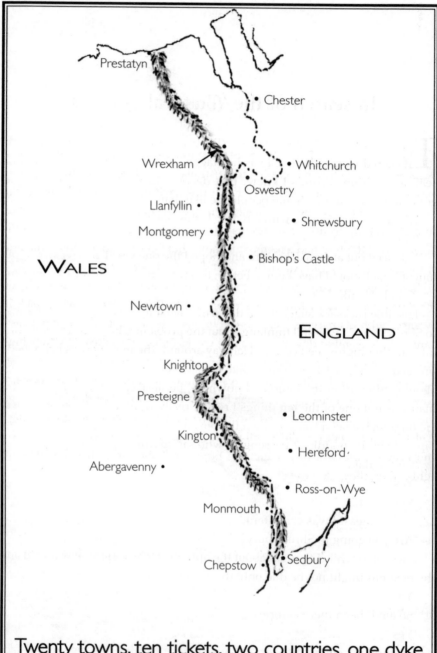

Twenty towns, ten tickets, two countries, one dyke

In search of the 'Cultural Quarter'

THE NEW PASSENGER'S TINY EYES, black as currants in a pale, soft face, flickered from side to side as he staggered down the aisle looking for a seat, and within seconds I knew, that despite thirty empty places, he was going to sit next to me. Some people are like that.

His accent was Scouse with a twist, 'Is this one taken?'

'No.'

I glanced out at rural Cheshire and hoped the one word answer would put him off, but I should have known better: this was a man who wanted company.

'Good. Thanks.'

His little rucksack suggested a day trip – what if he was going all the way to Shrewsbury? I was still thinking about the problem when our driver drifted into another high-speed corner. Halfway around, the newcomer's bulky body pressed me against the window like a specimen on a slide and I wondered about getting off in the middle of nowhere, because spending time with this man was not one of the ten things I really, really wanted to do before I died. He might have been staring down the bus, but I knew he was speaking to me rather than the huddle of passengers who sat up front.

'Cold today.'

'Yes.'

'Very cold.'

'Yes.' At least I was consistent.

'Are you going to Shrewsbury?'

I hesitated while I thought about the options. He was right, it was cold and the next bus might not be due until the spring.

'Yes.'

'So am I. Been there before?'

'Yes.'

He thought about that for a while, before turning his big, round face towards me and asking another question.

'Have you ever been to Warrington?'

'Yes.' He looked annoyed, as if I had just trumped his King.

'Ah … but have you ever been to Warrington's *cultural quarter?*'

'No.'

The man leant back in his seat with a small smile of triumph, while I thought about the reasons that had led me to this one-sided conversation with a dough-faced man on a bus bound for Shrewsbury.

A month or so earlier, as autumn retreated to leave the stage clear for its harder, colder brother, I had walked down a lonely hilltop lane, looked east towards Cheshire and thought about the border between England and Wales. Did it matter these days? A woman had once told me that there are people who think they are 'Border', rather than English or Welsh – was she right? Are there any real differences between the people who lived in towns on either side of the border, like Knighton in Wales and Kington in England? Are there any real differences in the towns themselves? The questions kept on coming. Has devolution in Wales begun to change things? Do people look across the border and like what they see?

What was stopping me finding out? Maybe there might even be a book in it somewhere. After all, it was not as if I was going to some remote country where natives still sent messages using cleft sticks and thought that one day Bruce Forsyth would crack the American market. It should be easy, but as I turned for home, I bumped into my first problem – how would I travel? Trains did not run to most of the places I wanted to visit and a car would keep me away from the people who, with luck, would give me wit and wisdom. By nightfall, the matter was settled – I would go by bus. That was it, I would use service buses to zig-zag back and forth over Offa's Dyke, from Prestatyn on the north Wales coast to Chepstow in the south and talk to fellow passengers and people in the towns and villages en route. What about calling it 'On an Offa Bus' or something similar? Yes, well, it sounded good to me anyway. I was on a roll, but then as vicious, lazy gusts of wind started to blow in from the general direction of Siberia, doubts began to surface.

Would anyone talk to me? Would they think I had escaped from the big house on the hill? Would it be easy to find out the times of buses? The last question turned out to be one the biggest problems of all. Throughout my journeys, I was to find that information about timetables for rural buses was usually given out on a 'need to know' basis. Well-meaning techno friends had a solution.

'Look it up on the web.'

Well I did, many times, and many times found last year's timetable, letters like NS, SO and XW, incomprehensible lines of numbers and strange symbols that could only be understood by people who can solve quadratic equations. Occasionally I phoned transport offices to be told that old Harry might be able to help, but unfortunately he was away from his desk looking for Lord Lucan. I knew I had to try other techniques. Have you ever tried getting information from one of those touch-screen displays? If you have, were you successful or were you arrested for battering the screen in frustration?

But all that angst lay ahead: it was time to make a start, because today was meant to be a practice run for the real thing. I opened a black notepad, took out my best biro, half turned towards the man who had been to Warrington's cultural quarter and asked my first question.

Prestatyn to Chester

I DID NOT SEE HIM AT FIRST, perhaps because the café was crowded with shoppers and the usual mixture of the idle and feckless enjoying a respite from the icy winds outside, but a more observant man would have noticed him, because he stood out like a conger eel in a tank full of fresh-faced innocent little goldfish. He had wet, pink lips. Wet, because his tongue emerged from time to time to touch them and pink to match the pink of his nails. His fingers rarely stayed still. In random sequence, they moved from fleshy thigh to the hair on wrists that squeezed out from tight cuffs and then up to the contours of a face that a friend of mine would have said was more pig than fox. He wore small John Lennon glasses with steel rims that hooked around close-set ears and a shiny charcoal black suit that might have impressed the local undertaker. But it was only when I glanced towards the windows and a threatening sky, that I felt the first frisson of alarm, because for some reason, a man with hot dark eyes was staring at me!

As I wondered whether to have another coffee, I felt like a tethered goat waiting to be eaten by someone on day release from a secure building surrounded by high walls. It was time to do some serious thinking: do not make eye contact with him, just go, it might be cold, but it's better than ending up as a hamburger. He is probably harmless but you never know. He might well have been harmless, but as it was the first day of a trip I wanted to complete in one piece, I left the café and walked to the beach. The man did not follow; perhaps he was a vegetarian.

Within ten minutes I had reached Offa's Dyke path, the long-distance walk that runs for nearly 180 miles through the borderlands of England and Wales. I stared at a tasteful black metal sign that marked the northern tip of the route and wondered how tiring and lonely it would be to walk the full length of the path which, in parts, follows the line of ditch and earthworks – Offa's Dyke, built by the king of Mercia in the last quarter of the eighth century. Why was it built? No-one quite knows, but one theory, that it was meant to discourage marauding Welsh tribes from making themselves at home in the flat, fat lands of Mercia and southern England, made sense to me. It might not have been a defensive barrier, but rather a statement of intent – west side you, east side us – we hope you understand.

Huddled out of the wind in the shelter of a shuttered lifeguard's hut, I stood and looked at the view. Against a background of dark sand and a grey–brown sea that reached the murky far away mountains of the Lake District, an elderly man and woman, both with red woollen hats, pinched faces and awkward stiff limbs, played ball with their laughing, squealing grandchildren, watched only by silent gulls and a man who was beginning to regret not wearing his warmest coat.

I hurried towards a nearby modern Tourist Information Centre, but found no staff inside a building which looked as if it had been closed for the long winter months when customers might be in short supply. The incident reminded me of those awful jokes told by men who inform you they 'went to Wales once – but it was closed!' I laugh every time I hear this – what wits they are! They see you washing your car and suggest you do theirs as well ... and if you're wearing a suit, they ask, 'what time is your interview?' They are the kind of men who squeal when they tell the television world that 'Anne Robinson is incredibly scary'. They are kind of pathetic.

Out at sea, dozens of windmills helped provide some of the electricity for the lights that blazed in an ugly modern building that lay just yards away. On the side that faced me, I could see a dozen drinkers in a brightly-lit bar and headed in their direction while a threatening squall headed in mine. Almost as soon as I walked inside, I saw a sign which told patrons that they could not use the restaurant unless they wore a top, but bare chests were OK for the adjoining bar. I pass on the information in case you are ever topless in Prestatyn.

A friendly barmaid served me a coffee as a dozen women drank and told jokes, while their toddler children, faces flickering from the colours of a giant flat screen television, ran around shouting and bringing joy into our lives. Charming as the scene might be, I wanted to scribble some notes and so side-stepped my way to an adjoining conservatory echoing to the sound of hard rain and sat down at a zinc-topped table. I did not mind finding the sticky, beery rings of glasses used by those who had passed this way before, because despite the noise of the downpour, the room was quieter than the bar I had left behind. Leaning back in my chair, I looked around and saw a plump teenager with a moist red face, wearing a white England football shirt, playing pool with a monosyllabic girlfriend, thin enough to have been used as the cue. Within touching distance, an increasingly desperate Brummie family were trying to decide what they might do later in the day. Occasionally, one of them would make a suggestion that would be vetoed immediately by a grandfather who possessed all the engaging charm of an East German figure-skating judge at the time when the Iron Curtain was a daily reminder of political realities.

For a few moments I fought depression as I listened to the sharp, savage words of people who wished they were back home in the Midlands and not trying to make the best of things on this wind-scoured part of the north Wales coast. I could imagine the thoughts of the increasingly desperate father of two sulky sons – boys please listen ... you have got to be positive ... it might be raining, bitterly cold, there's not much to do and your mother's in a mood, but we are on a mini break so let's start enjoying ourselves!

At the next table, a solitary, middle-aged man, with a half-empty pint in front of him, used a mobile phone to arrange accommodation for the night. A mother and daughter came out of the bar, opened a glass door a couple of yards away from me and blew the smoke from a shared cigarette into the tail end of the rain squall. Besides an enjoyment of smoking, the women seemed to have a lot in common. Both favoured discreet nose studs and skimpy vests of slightly different shades of pastel pink. Both wore jeans so tight that horizontal creases stood out like the rungs on a ladder. Both were overweight (apparently we're not allowed to say fat these days), both had lurid tattoos on fleshy arms and both swore in the same wonderfully uninhibited way. I looked past the women to the sign for the Offa's Dyke path and thought about evolution. Twelve hundred years after the dyke was built, a mother and daughter were swapping hazy memories about good nights they'd had and wondering if someone called Shane would be hung like a donkey. In evolutionary terms, twelve hundred years might be just the blink of an eye, but listening to the two women, evolution did not seem to be moving very fast.

Within minutes, the solitary man made a comment about the weather and we began chatting like old friends. It was only as he was telling me that he had just walked the whole length of the path, that I noticed his rucksack. Where had he stayed en route?

'Mainly B and Bs.'

'What if there weren't any around?'

'I camped.'

Fair play to him, because the man finishing his well-deserved beer was, at sixty-nine, more than ten years older than me, and originally from London. He had started walking after the warning of a heart attack, enjoyed it and now it had become a way of life. In recent years, he had knocked off long-distance walks around Pembrokeshire and England's south-west peninsula, thus putting my modest little daily strolls into proper perspective. How long had it taken him to complete Offa's Dyke path? He could not give me a quick answer, because he had lost track of time. Eventually, he told me it might have taken him twelve days. Twelve days for 180 miles! Had he miscalculated? He might be as fit as a butcher's dog, but twelve days? Yet he had the look of an honest man, and I believed him. Had he met any 'border' people? After a few seconds' thought, he gave me an answer.

'I *think* so, they just come from where they're born, not a country.'

'What do you mean?'

'I think it's something to do with the land, the people I'm talking about come from a valley or a village – they were born in a *place*, not England or Wales.'

'Where did you meet them?'

He smiled. 'In pubs, or B and Bs on farms.'

'Did you meet any Hampstead Hippies?'

His smile broadened; he knew what I meant.

'Yes, they're everywhere, met lots of them down in the West Country.'

'Living the good life, getting away from it all.'

'But not too far away from their parents' money!'

'That would *never* do.' For some reason I sounded like a ham actor auditioning for work.

He gave me a brief, friendly smile before looking at his watch and standing up. 'I'd better get going, I usually buy some little presents at the end of a trip – it's a sort of tradition.'

I handed him his rucksack. It was like lifting a small car and I wondered how he had managed to carry it up hills, across fields and down valleys, all the way from south Wales. It was time for me to leave as well; I had a bus to catch, but first I wanted to have another look around Prestatyn. It was a puzzling town. In the main street, there were two Welsh-language chapels, one of them next door to a big, bold and brash off-licence that seemed to have used up most of the world's known reserves of dayglow orange for the offers that shrieked from its windows. Just along the road, a couple of shops sold some quality designer clothes near a café where natural fibres had never knowingly been worn by customers. I wandered along the pavements and tried to absorb the atmosphere of the place. Towards the bottom of the hill, a knot of young women, dressed in skirts short enough for a summer's day, shivered as they stared down at mobile phones as if hoping to be told that Mad Bad Big Boy Ben was still interested in getting to know their minds. Their mothers chose from good-looking cuts of meat in the window of a traditional butcher, whilst a clutch of middle- aged men came out of a bookie's shop where any number of colour televisions showed several different sporting events at the same time. It was a scene which provided a cameo of some aspects of life in modern Britain as it approached the second decade of the twenty-first century and made me wonder what Prestatyn might have been like in its heyday.

Judging by old sepia photographs on the walls of a nearby café, it seemed to have been a serene and affluent place which nestled below attractive hills that overlooked a long, sandy beach where unending generations of waves saw their final moments. The photographs were dated 1917, when different generations – this time young men from every corner of the world, fought a war and lost their innocence or lives along the way, but sadly, the deaths and injuries did not stop in 1918, when the guns fell silent at eleven o'clock on the eleventh day of the eleventh month of the year.

An old friend of mine, Comrade G. J. Morgan, a military and aviation enthusiast, had once told me about a tragic event which took place at Kinmel Park Camp, just down the coast from Prestatyn, a few months after the end of hostilities. The camp was the scene of some heavy-duty rioting when battle-weary Canadian Army veterans turned on their officers. Against a background of a flu pandemic, the sheer frustration of not being shipped home from their north Wales transit camp, and the pointlessness of repetitive route marches during one of the coldest winters on record, led eventually to mutiny, injuries and deaths. These soldiers had lived through war, but died in peace. It was a sad, tragic footnote to a conflict that had changed the lives of so many people from all over the world.

In the same café, I spoke to a woman who was glad she had moved to the town from neighbouring Rhyl. Why?

'Rhyl's very rough, at least some of it is. We might get our share of troubles, but it's much better round here.'

She had been born in Lancashire, but had moved to this part of the north Wales coast in her early teens.

'A lot of people come from Liverpool or Wigan or wherever, that's why the accent's not really Welsh is it?'

'Do you think of Prestatyn as a Welsh town?'

'No, not like Bethesda or those places up in the mountains.'

She hesitated before speaking again, 'My children learn Welsh in school, I'm not sure why and I'm not sure they should.'

For a moment I thought about asking her a problematical question about compulsory Welsh in schools, but then decided to choose the safer option.

'If Wales play England, who do they want to win?'

'I'm not sure, but Wales I think.'

Her answer seemed to come as a surprise and I suspected that once she got home, she would put the same question to her children. For a few moments we chatted about living in the town while I geared myself up to face the cold world outside.

Luckily, it did not take long to reach the bus station and within minutes, I was peering at the timetable and glancing around in the hope of assistance. I *thought* the Chester bus would be along soon, but was not *sure* – there is a big difference, especially if you're freezing and wondering if the trip had been a good idea in the first place.

On one stand, a husband and wife, who had been married long enough for spontaneity to have disappeared like New Year's resolutions, started bickering as they stared unseeing at odd scraps of paper swirling high above the grey roofs of the town like a flock of demented sparrows. A few yards away, a teenage girl was still having problems lighting a cigarette in an anti-smoking wind when the Chester bus arrived. I had been right! It was a triumph for Swansea education, or more likely a bit of luck …

We had reached the green outskirts of Prestatyn, when the man, sitting next to me, started a conversation about a crossword puzzle he was trying to complete in a daily paper. He told me he was from Chester, but had positive opinions about Wales and the Welsh. Because of its rarity value, I will write that again. The man was from Chester, but had positive opinions about Wales and the Welsh! As our bus headed along a straight, flat road, the man, who was perhaps a few years older than me, smiled as he remembered teenage weekends riding his bike through the very different countryside that surrounded places like Llangollen or Abersoch. I was impressed for two reasons – firstly the fact that anyone could ride so far without performance-enhancing drugs, but mostly because he could pronounce both towns as if he had been born and brought up in them, we usually get Clangolen and Abersock. A friend of mine had once talked about the problems many non-Welsh men and women had pronouncing some villages in Wales, 'I don't mind them not getting it right, some places must be very hard to say, but I resent the fact they don't even *try* to make a decent attempt. In fact, they revel in getting it wrong!'

For the next few miles, the man from Chester told me about the job he had done before retirement and the years he had spent in the Middle East. It made for easy listening as our bus moved smoothly along a sinuous road, lined on one side by tall, overhanging trees. It was a nice, relaxed, undemanding conversation which gave me the occasional opportunity to glance northwards, beyond the narrow ribbon of industrial development to the distant sand dunes that formed the core of a Site of Special Scientific Interest. To me at least, it was an appealing juxtaposition – important flora within a short distance of big industrial sites like the major gas terminal we passed just before turning up the very steep hill that led to Holywell. It was time to get off the bus and spend a few hours in a town which, in my mind was linked, somewhat hazily, to a holy well and miracles.

But a few hours later, I was not much the wiser, so if you want more detail, I would suggest a town guide, the internet, or chatting to Myth Legend or some other lisping folklorist, because what mattered to me was the nature of the place and this particular place had the feel of a community. Despite the usual signs of modern Britain – pubs for sale, closed public toilets and blank-faced teenagers walking along staring down at mobile phones, the pedestrianised centre of Holywell appeared to be busy enough as people hurried in and out of warm shops. I should have worn my big coat. The gusts of wind made things worse. I had made a mistake and was paying for it.

On a bench, a man and a woman, each pushing seventy, sat leaning against each other like someone had gone mad with a glue gun. Both had the wiry bodies and wind-tanned faces of walkers and were wearing leaf-green anoraks that mocked the feeble efforts of the weather to make them feel a bit on the nippy side. Both smiled in my direction as I stood and wondered what to do next. I was struck by the fact that they alone seemed unperturbed by a wind that was now strong enough to cleanse the streets of strollers and posers. I decided to find out the secret of eternal warmth, and so, with a grunt of determination, I headed into the gale, wiped away my tears and sat down next to them. Just as I said, 'Cold today,' I remembered a strange conversation on a Shrewsbury-bound bus and wondered if Warrington's cultural quarter would be any warmer today. I made a mental note to investigate the possibilities of spending a long weekend there. It was a seductive image.

There was a momentary pause as the man considered my observation. 'Well … ' He was just being polite; to him it was probably a morning in May.

His wife plucked the green sleeve of her anorak, 'These are pretty good, they have to be.'

He explained why. 'We do a lot of walking.'

'We enjoy it.'

'We wouldn't do it unless we did!'

'Where do you walk ... around here?' They smiled like synchronised swimmers before the man answered my question.

'Sometimes, but mostly we get up in the hills because we ... '

'Love the views and the exercise.'

'It keeps us fit.'

'We haven't been ill for years not like ... '

'Those people who just sit around.'

'Watching television.'

'Playing bingo.'

'Or doing nothing.'

Did you keep up? For information, the woman had the last line as her husband nodded approval. Their timing was immaculate, but I wanted to ask about the border between England and Wales. Perhaps it would be best to approach down the blind side.

'Do you always walk in Wales?'

They glanced at each other for a moment before the woman took the lead.

'No, not always but ... '

As was becoming predictable, her husband completed the sentence and then asked a question of his own.

'Usually, why?'

I gave an early version of what was to become a standard reply about doing some research for my book, before the man spoke out of turn.

'A few weeks ago we went to look at some bogs near Whitchurch.'

'And Wrexham ... some bits were in Wales ... they were nature reserves ... they call them mosses.'

'They go across the border.'

'Because the border doesn't matter ... '

'If you're a butterfly.'

For a few seconds I said nothing as the two smiled placidly in my direction while I wondered how long a butterfly would survive on a day like this. Not long, but it was a striking end to the conversation. I wiggled my toes to prove they still existed, said goodbye and hurried back to the bus-stop. It was time to make the last push to one of the most visited small cities in the land – Chester.

Afternoon buses often have a different feel to them and this one was no exception. Most of the passengers seemed to be going home and chatted away quite happily as we headed back down the hill to the urban ribbon that runs from the border at Queensferry to the town of Flint. Two men sat across the aisle to me. Just as I wondered how I could start a conversation with them , the younger man, wearing a polo shirt with a British Aerospace logo, one of the area's biggest employers, stood up to go and my chance was lost. I wanted to ask him what he thought about the media using the phrase 'British Aerospace, Chester', when the factory was actually in Wales. He would probably have told me he could not care what it was called, as long as someone carried on paying him for doing his job.

The little episode represented what was to become a recurring problem on my travels – the difficulty of starting 'normal' conversations with total strangers who might, for some odd reason, be alarmed if a pen-wielding man in the seat in front turned around, gave them an encouraging smile, started asking questions, and then wrote down their answers. They would have some questions of their own … who was he? What did he want? Should I tell the driver?

I was still thinking of different opening conversational gambits, when we reached the handsome village of Hawarden, which, in the pale wash of a watery winter sun, looked as prosperous as a silver-haired duchess of independent means. I did not know at the time, but within yards, the journey was to take on a new dimension.

The attractive young blonde who boarded the bus from a stop half-way along the main street, was probably only a year or so out of her teens and dressed in layers of earth-coloured clothes made from natural fibres. She wore a leather bracelet which might have been a recent present from an Apaché boyfriend, and supple chestnut brown boots which looked as if they were bought in an upmarket shoe shop where prices are never displayed.

As our crawling line of traffic passed through the village, my new travelling companion started a conversation.

'Nice to see it nearly full.'

I came in half a beat late, so she added a helpful comment.

'The bus I mean.' Some of these old people are very slow.

'Yes.'

'I use buses a lot.' Her accent was educated London.

'Oh ... ' I nodded approvingly and wondered what else to say.

Her brow was furrowed. 'Don't you?'

'No, but I'm enjoying this trip, it's a good way of seeing the countryside.'

'It's a good way of saving the countryside.'

'Is it? How?'

I sounded like the old children's television programme; she sounded pleased to help me find the Path of Enlightenment. I had asked my questions as we waited behind a parked van while traffic came the other way. I fantasised about what I would like to do to those rude drivers who just sailed through and did not acknowledge the manners of the man behind our steering wheel. The fantasy included tattoos, public humiliation and just enough pain to make them think twice about doing it again. The thought cheered me up as the blonde pointed to the stream of passing cars, 'If all those people were in this bus, everyone would be better off.'

With a little smile I said, 'There wouldn't be enough room.'

'You know what I mean.'

'Yes, but sometimes cars are the only solution for people who ... '

She broke in before I could finish, 'Cars are never the solution, cars are always the problem. We need to get rid of them.'

We were moving again, driving past fields of serene, indifferent cows as I decided whether to call it quits and nod in agreement, or continue and get into a discussion which could get a bit edgy as we travelled the last dozen miles to our destination. It was no contest.

'Getting rid of cars might solve some problems, but cause others.'

'I need some examples.' In my experience, stern-faced blonde eco warriors always need examples.

'Well, lots of people want to go where buses don't ... cars give independence and as ... '

She cut me off with an indisputable truth, 'We wouldn't be talking if we were both travelling in separate cars.'

'That's true, but would it matter?'

'Of course it matters, we've all got to talk more.'

'About?'

'The environment, *our* environment, it's the only one we have ... and we're messing it up!'

'With cars?'

The young woman paused so that her words would have more effect, 'With cars, with planes ... with pollution ... with everything!'

'Maybe, but it's complicated, at least it is for me – you know things like climate change and ... '

She was in faster than Gareth Edwards at his best, 'Climate change is not complicated, not if you know the facts.'

'And you do?'

Her smile was satisfaction on warm, buttered toast, 'Yes.'

'Then you're lucky'.

I glanced through the windows at Broughton and the Cheshire Plain beyond, before adding a heartfelt comment, 'Most people are puzzled by it all.'

'Tell me what puzzles you.'

It was time to get some answers from someone who was lucky enough to know it all.

'Well, someone said that reusable nappies are worse than disposable ones, because the energy needed to wash them harms the environment more than putting them in a landfill site and ... '

She could not wait to break in, 'I'll deal with that one later.'

'Right, is it true that paper bags need more energy to manufacture and store than plastic bags?'

Her serene smile might have suggested inner peace, but her eyes sent out a very different message.

'Keep going.'

I had been round long enough to suspect she was playing for time while she thought up some answers. Sometimes even age has its benefits, although I cannot think of too many at the moment.

'A government minister admitted the environment would suffer less if everyone on a diesel train was given one of those big 4 x 4s ... think there's anything in it or was he just whipping himself in public?'

As we passed the Aerospace plant, she bought even more time by asking a question.

'Do you believe in global warming?'

'Do you mean do I think it exists?'

'Yes.'

Swansea schooldays flashed through my mind. 'Well, I only got as far as 'O' Level Biology, but from what you read, it's probably happening.'

'Probably! There's no probably about it, if we keep going the way we are, we'll all be dead in just over sixty years!'

Sixty years, that would mean I would be dead before I reached my one hundred and twentieth birthday! I needed to know more and the sooner the better.

'Just over sixty years, that sounds very precise.'

'It is. We've got some good people working on it.'

'Experts usually end up disagreeing ... anyway what about my questions? I'd like to know more so I can explain to other people.'

She gave me an exasperated look, which suggested she had her doubts about my efforts to help save the world.

'Is it worth it? Sounds like you've got a closed mind. I've told you what matters, that should be enough.'

I remembered six words written by Joseph Joubert, a near contemporary of Napoleon, 'Ask the young. They know everything.'

On my left, I saw a road sign which prompted another question.

'Ever been to Saltney Ferry?'

Her still stern face didn't change expression. 'No.'

The one word answer meant she was still annoyed with me. Should I tell her that I had Googled it and found that some websites had moved the Flintshire village into Cheshire? Saltney Ferry might have been in Wales, but half a dozen sites gave its address as Flintshire, Cheshire or Flintshire, Chester. Who moved it – someone trying to play mind games? Did the locals know? Did the locals care? Were the locals Welsh?

I glanced at the woman's pursed lips and moved seamlessly on to our destination of Chester. Did she like it?

'No, don't like towns.'

Then why she was going to one today?

'I'm meeting a friend at the railway station. She's from Nicaragua, got to Heathrow last night.'

'So she had to fly.'

There was a slight hesitation before the word escaped through gritted teeth.

'Yes.'

It was time for the surprisingly sensitive new me to let her come to terms with the shameful admission.

There was no fuss as we crossed the border into England. This was not the Demilitarised Zone that separated the two Koreas or the prickly line between India and Pakistan; this was such an invisible border that we were passing through Chester's suburbs before I realised we had left Wales behind.

For some reason, Chester has always reminded me of what Clive James once said about Adriano Panatta, the Italian tennis star of the seventies, 'He's good looking if you like your ice-cream runny.' The problem is I do not. Many people swoon as soon as someone mentions Chester, but for whatever reasons, the city with the warm complexion has always left me cold. Tourism might be big business these days, but those places that trade on it are not always my kind of place. Each to his own and all that ...

Just after we passed a big brown sign that told us we were entering an 'International Heritage City', and headed towards one of the bridges that span the Dee, I thought about the questions I would like to ask the eco–warrior sitting next to me: Did she live in a shack made out of recycled rubbish? Did she wash her clothes in a stream? Did she have a computer and if she did, was it solar powered? Did she use a mobile phone? Did she read newspapers made using electricity? By the time we reached the city side of the bridge, I had decided the Yes/No vote was probably 50/50. Deadlock became gridlock thanks to a broken down car and traffic lights that had not turned up for work. I sat next to the still silent young woman and thought about the problems of living modern lives in ways entirely compatible with our beliefs. But then, as we crawled through the city's streets, I remembered one of my favourite Groucho Marx quotations that seemed to fit the bill: 'These are my principles, and if you don't like them ... well, I have others.'

When the bus reached its destination, my leather-booted travelling companion stood up, stared down at me, shook her head slowly from side to side, and then said in a voice of doom, 'Just over sixty years ... ' I nodded, smiled, and hoped I would be so lucky.

Over the centuries, for whatever reasons, Chester and nearby Wrexham, have never become joined at the hip. Although the relationship might have changed from the days when Chester played a key role in keeping a bellicose people at arm's length, some underlying principles have not. The fact that a law, still apparently on the statute books or whatever they are called, permits those Welshmen found within the city walls after sunset, to be shot with a crossbow, suggests that the towns, less than a dozen miles apart, and of roughly similar size, have a problematic relationship. But not all cross border relationships appear to be so problematical.

In recent years, local authorities on both sides of Offa's Dyke have been working on a 'West Cheshire North East Wales Sub Regional Spatial Strategy'. Those used to playing Bullshit Bingo, will not be surprised to find the strategy's near 130-word vision statement, written in just one amazingly long sentence, is littered with terms like – economic growth intertwined with the need to realise social inclusivity, competing in the regional, national and global market place, facilitate, sustainable development – and the rest of the usual suspects. As might have been foreseen, a number of people, especially those living in Wrexham, Flintshire and Denbighshire, have real concerns about the initiative, and wonder what is in it for Wales. One opponent of the strategy recently expressed his fears if it ever becomes a coherent reality.

'I'm all for sensible planning and co–operation between local authorities, but this is just an attempt to get rid of the border and merge north-east Wales with north-west England.'

He was also worried about the strategy's intention to bring about benefits to the 'Liverpool city–region' as it is called in the report. 'Why? What's in it for us? What's in it for Wales? It has never been made clear – some of us think it just means more commuter towns in Wales built as close as possible to the M53.'

But not every opponent is Welsh. One Chester-based academic had told me his major concern is the way 'things are being done, there doesn't seem to be any proper debate about it all … it is unaccountable planners and puffed up bureaucrats indulging themselves.' Watch this space as they say.

Did I say towns earlier? Sorry, I forgot Chester is a city, but to me cities are huge, sprawling places, full of imposing buildings, specialist hospitals and suburbs big enough to be towns in their own right and Chester is not – it is nothing personal; all those 'cathedral' cities come into the same category. While sweetness and light might be in short supply where the Cheshire Plain meets the uplands of Wales, negative stereotypes appear to thrive in the minds of at least some of the people who live in the area.

Years ago, I asked three nearly middle-aged Welshmen, two of whom came from Wrexham, to give me some words to describe Cheshire's famous county town. They had played rugby for Wrexham and remembered Chester refusing to offer a fixture on sporting grounds – in essence, Wrexham would not be able to give them much of a game. Didn't they know that Chester Rugby Club had a long and glorious history? Eventually after repeated requests from the Welsh club, Chester graciously consented to a game provided it was at home. Apparently, Wrexham won by more than forty points. For some reason, the fixture was not repeated.

This background might have helped shape their response which was based on words and phrases like English snobs, rich bastards etc ... I think you get the idea.

When writing this chapter I spoke to a young married couple from Chester, to ask them what came to mind when Wrexham was mentioned. He was the first to answer.

'Well ... Wales I suppose, and ... ' While he hesitated, his wife came in.

'Coal and steel ... think they used to make it there.' She smiled. 'It would have been easier if you'd said Wales instead of just Wrexham.'

'Alright, give me some words for Wales.'

It didn't take long before they were taking it in turns to answer.

'Cardiff ... rugby.'

'Mountains ... sheep.'

'Beaches ... fantastic beaches.' The woman had turned to her husband for confirmation. 'Harlech's our favourite, isn't it?'

He smiled as good memories came back to him. 'Yes, it's great ... my turn ... right, what about singing? Lots of choirs – Tom Jones.'

'People speaking Welsh.'

She turned to her husband. 'Remember that pub outside Portmadoc when we went with Viv and Ian?'

He made a face, and then gave me an explanation. 'Yes, our friends didn't like the locals speaking Welsh when we came in, especially Ian.'

'Viv wasn't too happy either.'

I looked at them. 'What about you two? How did you feel?'

The young man had turned towards his wife. 'We didn't mind, did we?'

'No course not, they were speaking their own language in their own country, what's wrong with that?'

Her husband had added more detail. 'I told Ian he wouldn't expect everyone in a French bar to stop speaking French if he walked in.'

I was curious to know Ian's response. 'What did he say to that?'

'He just said it was different because everyone in Wales can speak English, but they can't in France.'

'I said that wasn't the point, but I don't think he understood.'

After thanking the nice fair-minded couple, I started pounding the streets of Chester looking for this Ian, but it was to be an unsuccessful mission. Perhaps I should have asked them what he looked like.

Buildings might have taken the edge off the vicious wind, but the late afternoon chill sharpened it again as I walked up some steps to the upper level of Rows. For those who have never heard of the Rows, do not worry, help is at hand. Let me quote from a tourist brochure written by someone who had just discovered alliteration.

Browse two tiers of blissful boutiques and beguiling balconies encased in medieval majesty.

Later, in a busy café, I enjoyed a blissfully hot cup of tea and read more purple prose about the city … 'From Roman sandals to killer heels, Chester effortlessly blends centuries of substance with rolling acres of style.'

I looked up as an elderly, whiskery pensioner who sported a dew drop at the end of a long red nose, sat down at the table opposite, and wondered if he knew he was about to eat a slice of fruit cake in a city which can be 'quietly dignified or outrageously glamorous.' Who writes this sort of stuff? Do they really believe it themselves? All over Britain, glossy brochures are being mass produced saying things like 'the site is an elegant reminder of a past built on a rich heritage of sacrifice and the need to track time in all its timeless forms'. We are talking about Stonehenge in case you were wondering. After reading through the last few pages, you might think I really don't like Chester, but I would urge you not to make up your mind until I deal with the contentious issue of town criers.

Over the years, I have come to realise that there are some people who like them, just as there are some people who like clowns, Noel Edmunds, sitting in traffic jams and sticking pins in their eyes. My understanding is that Chester is the only place in Britain to have retained the historic tradition of *regular* proclamations being made by burly, bearded (alliteration can be catching) men, who ring a bell and shout the latest news in cod Shakespeare while looking for photo opportunities from visitors who might help them get a part in a television costume drama. We make up our minds about places in an instant. Decisions are made about places on the tiniest scraps of experience and I suspect it will always be the same. For example, the first time I ever visited Chester, I stood on a pavement near the Cross and listened to a tubby man, dressed in some sort of long cutaway coat with the usual gold braiding, ringing a hand bell, and then bellowing away to everyone who passed. I did not have a choice; only the deaf managed to avoid the witless words of the bearded buffoon.

Memories of that sunny summer's day and the strength of my feelings came back to me. Nothing had changed since that moment when, on the flimsiest of evidence, I began forming an opinion about the chocolate-box city on the banks of the Dee. A few months later that opinion had been confirmed, when a lecturer colleague, who had been brought up in a comfortable part of Chester, hesitated when I suggested he and his wife come round for a meal.

'At your place?'

'Yes.'

'In Wales?'

'Yes.'

'Well, it might be ... uh...'

Things had gone silent for a moment or so as he tried to find the right words. Somehow I knew what was coming.

'Well ... uh ... thanks ... but look, we're having some people over for supper in a few weeks' time, you'd be *very* welcome to join us ... we can always come to you again ... you know, when the weather is better ... perhaps in the spring.'

I had tried to make a joke of it.

'When the snowdrifts have melted on the upper slopes of Marford Hill ...'

He had given me an uncertain smile. 'Yes, I suppose so.'

Thinking back, the conversation must have taken place on one of my grown-up days, because I accepted his offer.

His halting words might have shuddered and stopped, but my brain had begun to work on plans to turn Chester into a giant industrial estate, where beards were banned and every penny of profit was sent across the border to Wales. Now, years later, I was looking forward to criss–crossing the same border from north to south and making similar rational judgements about places that found themselves on different sides of Offa's Dyke.

It was time to blend into the gathering darkness that was beginning to wash over the city and walk back to the bus station for the return journey to the bright lights of Prestatyn.

Wrexham to Whitchurch

ALTHOUGH IT WAS EARLY on in my journey, I suspected that little old ladies do not have to look at timetables. They stand at a bus stop and *know* that the 8.15 will be four minutes late because of road works, but then smile and tell you not to worry, 'because the driver will make up the time.' They use buses every day and for some, the bus has probably taken the place of family. For them, familiarity has not bred contempt, but reassurance. They are not the kind of people who love studying timetables; they do not need to, because buses would be their specialist subject on *Mastermind*.

Timetable junkies are different. Timetable junkies actually *enjoy* looking down little columns of figures and working out if they can make the connection to Minsterley. It doesn't matter if they are going by bus, train, boat or plane or combinations thereof – what matters to them is the process – the analysis, calculation, breaking of the mystery codes that make working out timetables so difficult for people like me. To them, happiness is studying railway timetables for the Basque country and planning complex weekend journeys when there is an 'r' in the month. They understand at a glance the mysteries of a timetable, but people like me usually stare at the figures in hopeless desperation. And please remember, that if you ever talk to one, these people still wear digital watches with a quiet sense of pride. My advice is to avoid them wherever possible, but it did not look as if I would need to today, because from a first, quick inspection, there were no junkies on board the bus to Whitchurch.

With luck, I would enjoy the journey. The signs were good. The morning showed glimpses of sunny promise, we had a polite, smiling driver, the back seat was mine and, judging by the little bursts of conversation I overheard, most of the handful of passengers seemed to know and like each other. This was a world away from a big city late night bus filled with tense civilians and foot soldiers from teenage gangs; this was a place where manners still mattered.

Before the trip, I had spoken to a number of people who had been born and raised in Wrexham and been told that the town was changing fast. It was not just developments like the nearly completed Eagles Meadow retail and residential centre which we passed as we headed towards Marchwiel, the first big village en route, but in other, less obvious, ways.

A lecturer at the town's college had said that Wrexham was now more 'Welsh' than it used to be. 'Maybe you don't hear the language so much, but there's a lot more signs of Welshness around these days.'

'Such as?'

'Oh you know, flags, bilingual signage ... those kinds of things.'

'Things that tell visitors they're in another country?'

'Yes, I suppose so.'

Some of the trappings might have been imposed as the result of laws passed by the Assembly Government in Cardiff, but no-one made locals buy 'Wales' or 'Cymru' stickers for the parked cars we were passing ... no-one made the little group of teenagers standing on a street corner on this bright, cold morning, buy the red Welsh rugby or Wrexham football jerseys they were wearing. These visible symbols of allegiance to nation or town were worn through choice and I knew that nowadays, football matches with neighbouring Chester City often started around noon, to try and reduce the chance of trouble between rival fans. Local derbies are usually competitive, but the national dimension made things worse. Wrexham, less than ten miles from the English border, might not return a nationalist MP, but it was in Wales and felt Welsh.

Wrexham, less than ten miles away from the English border, might not return a Nationalist MP, but it was in Wales and felt Welsh. As some new passengers boarded, I thought about a recent conversation with a good-natured man in his mid thirties who had been born and brought up on the Chester side of the town. I'd told him that to me Wrexham didn't seem to be some sort of border hybrid, but definitely 'Welsh.' Did he agree?

He considered the matter for a few seconds. 'Yes, probably, but a lot of people have moved to Wrexham lately ... especially around this bit and that might change things.'

Were we talking about newcomers from places like Portugal and eastern Europe?

'No not really ... I think some of those will work in Wrexham for a bit and then go home ... no I was mainly thinking about the English ...lots have them have settled here ... I've got nothing against them but ...'

'But what?'

A smile had touched his eyes as he repeated my question. 'But what ... yes ... what do I mean?'

I smiled back. 'You tell me!'

'I don't know ... it's difficult to explain.'

After a few seconds he thought of something. 'Let me give you an example. I went to a local pub once to watch the football; Wales were trying to qualify for the European championships ...'

The words had driven my smile away to wherever smiles go to hide. 'We're always trying to qualify for the European Championships or the World Cup ...'

For a couple of minutes we chatted about the problems faced by the smaller nations thanks to a seeding system which helped ensure the bigger countries usually got through their qualification group. You have to think of viewing figures and advertising revenues – but back to the pub.

'England were playing at the same time ... the landlord was English ... a lot of the people in the bar were English so ...'

'You watched the England game?'

'Yes ... from time to time someone flicked over so we could see how Wales were getting on.'

'Was there any argument about it?'

'No, not really ... a few of us weren't happy but ... it would probably be different in other pubs.'

There was a moment's pause while he thought. 'Maybe in Brymbo, Brynteg, Coedpoeth, places like that."

What did he mean?

'In some places there might have been an argument ... depends where you go. t's like the rugby^... when Wales beat England at Twickenham a few years ago, a couple of us watched it in a pub in the middle of town ...'

He smiled again at the memory. 'There didn't seem to be any England supporters around that day!'

Was he a Nationalist?

'No, never voted Plaid ... it's just sometimes you get a feeling of being a bit overwhelmed ... even if they're nice, because there's millions of them and not many of us!'

I was still thinking about the way a border affects some people when we swooped up the hill on the outskirts of Marchwiel under a sky which was losing its early promise. As we began to slow for the 30 mph sign, I remembered what I had been told by a friend of mine, who sings in a Chester choir. Apparently, English colleagues usually said they were going 'into' Wales, almost as if it was a trip into the unknown of a strange and foreign land. Were they typical? The journey might help me find out.

The slim woman, wearing dark trousers and fawn anorak who stood waiting for the bus outside trim bungalows with gardens put to bed for winter, had short iron-grey hair and a ruddy, fresh face that had not seen make-up for some time. She signalled for the driver to stop with the precise movement of someone who knew her rights and then, even though she had left middle-age well behind, boarded with the quick movement of a young girl impatient to meet her friends. With a pleasant smile, she nodded greetings to the driver and trotted down the swaying aisle before sitting at the other end of the back seat. Within a hundred yards, she saw me trying to scribble in my open notebook that refused to stay still on this moving platform and asked a question.

'What are you writing about?'

While I wondered how much detail to give her, the woman saw the trouble I was having writing anything legible and said, 'When was the last time you were on a bus?'

This time I did not hesitate.

'Yesterday.'

She nodded as if it confirmed something she knew already, and then went back to her original question.

'What are you writing about?'

Her voice was quite low-pitched. If pushed, I would have guessed that she had been born in a leafy Home Counties village, but somewhere along the line, other parts of the world had left their mark.

'The people who live close to the border between England and Wales ...'

It was her turn to do some thinking.

'Don't you think it's strange we usually say the countries in that order?'

'What, England and Wales?'

'Yes.'

For some reason, I felt stupid. A smile had reached her clever, bird-bright eyes before she spoke again.

'Very few people refer to Wales and England; it doesn't really *go*, does it?'

I had always wanted to use the words of Evelyn Waugh's Mr Salter in a context like this and say 'Up to a point', but something made me give a one word answer.

'Possibly.'

Once again, a brief smile flitted over that scrubbed, healthy face, 'I can see I might have touched a raw nerve!'

She hesitated, as if it was her turn to choose her words with some care. I looked through the windows at the last of the morning's frost glittered in a stray burst of sun that shone down on pale fields and waited for her to speak again.

'I've never heard a Welsh man or woman, who live in Wales, say they're going to *England* for the weekend.'

'Neither have I.'

'They say they're going to Bristol or the Norfolk Broads or somewhere … they're going to a place.'

'Yes.' She was right. Did it come from some sort of ethnocentric perception of the world outside England?

'So why do lots of English people say they're going to Wales?'

I said I had a vague theory, but did not really know. Then, for a few moments, I thought about the conversation we had just had. Was it profound? Probably not, but then books like this are meant to be held together by the glue of perceptive comment and you have to start somewhere. We were bowling along a clear flat road and were in sight of the attractive weathered stone bridge at Bangor-on-Dee before she asked another question.

'Met anyone interesting on your travels?'

'You.'

The woman laughed, but she was.

In Bangor-on-Dee, a grandmother, daughter and toddler boy climbed aboard in a confusion of limbs, shopping bags, encouragement and the problems of collapsing a folding push-chair. The driver smiled. No-one became impatient. It was not that kind of bus. As we pulled away, I looked at the blushing red of the village's sandstone church and wondered if I would ever have the skill to describe the colour to a blind man.

The interesting woman wore her label lightly, but she still had a tiny pleased expression on her face as she took a diary from an inside pocket of her anorak and stared at the pages with the concentration I thought she would probably give to most things. She was still studying hard as we passed the racecourse and I wondered if her money had ever added to a bookie's retirement fund. I doubted it; this was not a woman who would bet on things beyond her control.

'Are you Welsh?' She was also a curious woman.

'Yes.'

'You sound it, but not all of them do.'

Them ... she was straying into sensitive areas again. While I wondered if my skin was too thin for a journey like this, we reached Overton – the pleasant village, quiet on a weekday morning when most commuters had probably left for office jobs in county towns half an hour's drive away through this rich border countryside. As fields became houses, I saw what looked to be a new sign which proclaimed that the village was twinned with La Mourette, wherever that is, and wondered if the link was active these days. I knew of twinning links that still flourished while others had died with people who had once kissed cheeks, shook hands and then signed a document promising to develop good relationships with their new friends from another country. Ideally, these relationships would be platonic, because although cross border sexual liaisons might help bring about one twinning aim – that of 'bringing people closer together', they do not usually do much for domestic harmony.

Overton did not look particularly Welsh, but what was I expecting – a male-voice choir walking down the main street singing about life underground in four-part harmony? Things had changed; the world had moved on while outsiders watched *How Green is my Valley*. In quick succession, we passed a balti house, the Jess E. James Nail and Hair Salon and shops where exotic products were sold to people called Williams and Jones. The bus swung left as I read 'Cocoa and Reading Rooms 1890' picked out in brick on the front of the Overton Recreational Club and heard the woman's apology.

'I hope I didn't offend you.'

'You didn't.'

'Good, I'm glad ... the problem is that most Welsh people are such easy targets.'

'What do you mean?'

'Anyone can do their accent for a start.'

'Well a stage accent, a sort of all-purpose Welsh accent, a voice that goes up and down like valley sides.'

She gave me a little smile that told me not to be so naïve. 'The people who imitate Welsh accents aren't the kind to worry too much about authenticity.'

I thought about it and agreed. 'You're right, all they've got to do is throw in a few things we don't actually say, like ... '

'Indeed to goodness or look you ... '

'Then talk about rain, sheep and rugby.'

There was a puzzled look on her face as she said, 'Why do they always seem to bring sheep into it?'

'It probably makes them feel better about their own miserable sex lives.'

She paused for a few seconds before saying, 'It's pretty insulting really, why do you put up with it?'

'Welsh people?'

'Yes.'

It was my turn to smile. 'We don't always.'

And so we continued like a slick double act until I stood up to go. We had reached Penley. Even though rain now seemed very near, it was time to leave the cosy bus and look around. Her final words as we parted were in keeping with the woman. I asked her what she thought of the village.

'Nice people, strange place.'

At first glance, the woman was at least half-right; Penley was strange. I had driven through it many times before, but had not really noticed that it did not seem to have a centre. Dark brick, two-storey houses were set well back from the main road that passed a church at the beginning of the village and a pub at the end, and although it had two schools, it did not seem to be a place where children would thrive. Yet I was probably being unfair. I had been in the village for less than a minute and I was already making huge generalisations, based on a few vague hurried feelings. Yet most of us reach quick conclusions about all sorts of things. We start watching a film and within seconds decide if it is going to be any good. We make firm judgements about houses, songs, meals, drinks, books, people and places almost as soon as we are introduced to them.

We do it all the time – we are human. I was human and probably wrong. Penley might well have been a place where children loved to live.

An intelligent and knowledgeable man, who had lived in the area for many years, suggested that any attempt to understand the history and nature of the village should start at the church. If at all possible, I try to listen to bright, knowledgeable people, so I walked to the edge of the village, opened the gate and stood looking at a graveyard that seemed old and tired under the tiny droplets of rain that were now beginning to fall from a sky as grey as school socks. Before I started up the path, I turned, looked across the road and saw the Madras School with its locally famous, thatched roof. I had heard its academic record was good, but I was a bad man for reaching a premature conclusion and so I made a gentle, mental apology for what I had thought earlier.

Not far from the path, one of the most prominent memorials carried the inscription, 'To the Glory of God and to the honoured memory of the men of Penley who gave their lives in the Great War 1914–1919'. It was the first, but would not be the last time I would see 1919 on memorials up and down the border, and I wondered about the date as I looked at another quotation underneath.

Live then for England
We for England died.

Things were different then. On modern war memorials, 'England' would be replaced by something else – perhaps the 'United Kingdom' or the 'Country' and, while the village might be close to the border, it was still in Wales. Then I had another thought; perhaps at the time the words were chiselled, England was probably shorthand for all the countries on these islands. Words change meaning through the years. For a few moments I thought about conflicts now being fought in Iraq and Afghanistan. Politicians, justifying intervention, would say troops were fighting for democracy, freedom or some abstract ideal, but I doubted if they would say to the bereaved families of troops killed in action, that their sons and daughters had died 'fighting for England'. Things were different then.

Later, in the same graveyard, I spoke to a formidably bright woman who seemed to have a clear, firm opinion on everything. The conversation drifted onto the same topic and very soon I learned that our young men and women who had been killed in Iraq and Afghanistan had 'died fighting for America.' She gave me the information as an established fact and, as we parted I knew that, unlike me, some people have no room for doubts in their purposeful existences.

Next to the old red sandstone church, there was a notice saying that I was in a 'wildlife area', where grass was only cut twice a year. In the porch I read a brief financial statement which showed that expenditure far exceeded income and thought that creating a wildlife area was probably making a virtue out of a necessity. Then, around the back of the church, I found the graves I had been told about. Polish graves which had been dug for men and women who died, not in their homeland, but in Wales. It did not take long to realise that although many of the deaths dated from the years of austerity that followed the Second World War, others were much more recent. For the next few minutes, I wandered around looking at the sad headstones, now slashed by wet rivers of rain, and wondered about the lives of the people who were buried here. Some must have been born in colliery towns or rural hamlets where buildings cuddle up for warmth in the winds that sweep in from Russia, but I knew that children were buried here as well – children who might have had a Polish mother, but who had never known the land of her birth; these were children whose short little lives had begun and ended in Wales.

I had been told that the Poles of Penley had come from a variety of backgrounds. Some were troops who had fought the Germans, others were refugees, or those freed from Stalin's camps, but most were doctors, nurses and other workers from the Polish Hospitals who ended their peripatetic existences in this village that lay about halfway between Wrexham and Whitchurch. After the relief and joy at the ending of the war, many thought that they would be going back to Poland, but the iron curtain soon clanged down and changed all that, so they carried on living in old army huts until they died or moved away. As their black-clad numbers dwindled and the millennium approached, I wondered what they would have felt if they knew that they would soon be joined by the first wave of Polish plumbers. The thought lightened my mood, but as I turned to leave the damp graveyard, darker feelings flooded back as I thought about the lottery of life and the harsh realities of death.

I walked to the pub past an industrial estate that would not help Penley's chances of winning 'Britain's Most Lovely Village' competition, and a school where the issues surrounding the teaching of the Welsh language had once produced a number of very angry parents. Apparently, some of them did not want their children to have to learn Welsh for the first few years at secondary level and had argued their case with real determination. A few even tried to have this part of Wrexham Local Authority, 'transferred' to Shropshire or Cheshire, but their efforts were doomed to failure. Although at times through the centuries, the border might have shifted about a bit, that was then and this was now and they were always going to lose the struggle. So Welsh became a core subject in the lower school and at least some of the school's website is now bilingual, and even if those at either end of the argument were not happy, I guessed that the compromise probably worked for most people. Maybe time had smoothed out the problems in this particular case, but, as I was going to find out, language issues still provoked resentment and anger in individuals, organisations and communities on either side of Offa's Dyke.

To me at least, the area did not look or feel as if it was a part of Wales, and I knew from the 2001 census returns that, as might be expected from its position hard up against the English border, the percentage of Welsh speakers was very low. But throughout Wales, even in places like this, numbers were growing. Now, although the country is a linguistic patchwork, nearly 30% of the population of Wales possesses at least one or more skills (speaking, reading, writing and understanding) in the Welsh language. The figures tell us that the highest percentage of Welsh speakers live in the north and west, where roughly 70% of the population claim to be fluent, but further south and east, numbers drop to less than 10%.

Oddly enough, these days it is not the rural heartlands that show the biggest growth of Welsh speakers, but urban centres and the old industrial valleys of south Wales. A few weeks before, an Australian had asked me what I thought about the chances of survival for the Welsh language. I told him that given how close we were to conurbations in the Midlands and north-west England, together with the seemingly unstoppable surge of media-driven English, the recent growth of the language has, to me at least, been a minor miracle.

A few yards ahead, I saw a teenager with coarsely-streaked blond hair and wearing an old combat jacket waiting for the next bus to Whitchurch, and wondered whether I should ask him a question. I wanted to know whether

Penley faced Wrexham to the west or Whitchurch to the east, but in these days of 'stranger danger', and in the light of some of my experiences on the trip so far, I was quite prepared to be ignored or told where to go. On this occasion I was lucky; he must have felt confident that I had not escaped from somewhere where they remove all your sharp objects.

The young man took his time answering as he thought about the question.

'I think it depends where you're from or what you think you are.'

'What do you mean?'

I didn't say anything as he searched for the right words to use.

'If you're Welsh, then you probably look to Wrexham and if you're not ...'

While he hesitated, I finished for him, 'You look to Whitchurch.'

But I had leapt in too early. He laughed as he signalled for the familiar bus to stop.

'No, I was going to say I feel sorry for you!'

Just a few miles from an unremarkable border, it was a surprising place to meet my first youthful Welsh Nationalist. He was still smiling as I watched the bus leave and began walking along an empty pavement to the pub. Apart from the lack of shutters, it might have been a deserted village somewhere off the beaten track in rural France. I wanted a drink, but I was going to be thirsty. I wanted a snack, but I was going to be hungry – the pub was closed. It looked like Penley had missed out on the Government's optimistic attempt to bring Continental café culture to modern Britain by all-day binge drinking and happy hours. Perhaps the Arts Minister's dream of the masses watching La Traviata on giant flat-screen televisions, while sipping fine wines, will come true and maybe, in years to come, outside smoking areas will not echo to the sound of community coughing, but to impassioned arguments about Jean Paul Sartre, yet the cynic within me had his doubts. I know you have got to give these initiatives a chance, but, as I stood trying the locked door, the Continent seemed a long way away.

Luckily, there is a good bus service between Wrexham and Whitchurch, and less than an hour after rattling the closed doors of the pub, I resumed my journey. As we left Penley behind, I saw the signpost for the little village of Welshampton and remembered the time I had been there before. It had been an afternoon like this, with softly weeping skies and a capricious wind that swept raindrops into my face as I had searched for the grave of a young African prince in the grounds of a Gilbert Scott church. The grave had taken some finding, the worn and faded lettering had seen to that, but I had used a mobile phone to contact an old friend to find out the grave's location, confident he would be able to help. He was and soon, thanks to his inimitable blend of accuracy and poetry, I was looking down at the last mortal resting place of Prince Jeremiah Moshueshue of Basutoland, now known as Lesotho by the likes of you and me.

The prince, a theological student, had been sent by his father, the king, to this country for further study, but, on a visit to Welshampton in 1863, to attend the consecration of the church of St Michael and All Angels, he had caught pneumonia and died. Poignantly, his was the first funeral to be held there. Once, many years ago, I had paid a brief visit to Lesotho and the sharp-edged memories of that odd, desiccated kingdom were still fresh within me. Before the journey, I had read that the nation's motto was *Khotso, Pula, Nala* or 'Peace, Rain, Prosperity'. Now, as our bus meandered through this prosperous countryside on the borders of Wales, I thought it ironic that it had been raining on the prince's grave for the best part of 150 years and hoped that somewhere he was at peace.

By the time we turned off the main road for the detour to Hanmer, our penultimate stop before Whitchurch, the rain had stopped, the sun had come out again, and I knew a bit more about the reasons passengers used the bus. Some, like the helpful retired couple sitting near me, were going to Whitchurch to shop in the town's supermarket that stood within yards of the bus station.

Why have the hassle of a car? Why not let someone else drive? And besides, not everyone could drive anyway. It made perfect sense, fewer cars on the road meant it was less harmful to global warming – any listening Green Guru would have been pleased, if only for a few hours. After that, their happiness would disappear like snow retreating through rising temperatures caused by the selfish actions of other people. For Green Gurus, happiness never lasts for long.

Those who soak the labels off their old tins before recycling them or cut open a tube of toothpaste to use the last few scrapings, are best avoided if you enjoy the company of cheerful people. Green Gurus are never ever truly happy, especially as they get ready for an appearance on primetime television where they tell the watching millions about their latest short list of do's and don'ts ...

- do become self sufficient like me in my Hampstead home where I live with my mega rich banker husband, twin girls, two boys and assorted pets ...
- do listen to people like me who know what is best for you ...
- do throw that apple core into the grass at the side of the road where it will degrade naturally ...
- do not watch television, because that uses too much electricity, unless there is a programme about me
- do not shop in supermarkets because that will add to the problem of global warming, and do please remember food miles when you are shopping
- do shop in a local butchers, the meat might cost a lot more than most supermarkets, but you will benefit from the knowledge that you are doing the right thing ...
- do stop and think before you decide to have more than two children ...

Confused? You will not be if you buy my book to help me pay for that Hampstead home and environmentally-sensitive holidays in places like Gstaad, Barbados and our house in Provence where we collect rainwater in a big barrel. Listening to myself, I decided I was becoming a grumpy old man, but no, that was not accurate, I was a grumpy old man *already* ...

Hanmer looked like one of the least rebellious places on earth. It nestled next to a little lake, or mere as it was called in these parts, and wore a look of tranquillity in the increasingly bright sunshine that made the village even more attractive. But in the minds of historians and nationalists at least, Hanmer was associated with rebellion. I got off the bus outside the imposing church of St Chad's, where Margaret, daughter of Sir John Hanmer, Chief Justice of the King's Bench in Westminster, had married Owain Glyndŵr, a man who will always be linked to the struggle for Welsh freedom. But this book is not the place to write about rights and wrongs, treachery, battles, blood and a legacy that can still affect the things some Welsh men and women say and do. Besides, other people have already written such books with skill and knowledge I could only dream about.

One of the helpful leaflets I found inside the church told me it was not the only time the village felt the pain of violence. In 1644, Nantwich Roundheads desecrated St Chad's, an act which caused outrage for men like Sir Thomas Hanmer who, together with other Welsh Royalists, ambushed the raiding party near the mere that today stretched peacefully in front of me, as I stood amidst the mellow stones in the neatly kept graveyard. The Cavaliers carried the day, but lost the war, and Sir Thomas was banished to France for three years, where he made good use of his time by studying the gardening methods of the French, Dutch and Italians. Informed sources tell us that he made a significant contribution to the development of formal gardens that many of us like to see and visit. My advice is to store that away in case you ever get asked it in a quiz. Other leaflets described people and events which had shaped the village and later, as I strolled across the quiet road to the shop cum post office, I wondered how many locals were aware of the rich history that surrounded them. Probably not many, if my own background was any yardstick. I grew up in a place where too many Swansea Jacks thought that Dylan Thomas was just the name of a pub.

As usual, I lurked between the aisles, pretending to choose something to eat, while waiting for the opportunity to pounce on anyone with an opinion about the border. This time I was lucky and before too long, I was talking to the friendly woman behind the counter who was from the north Wales coast. I asked about local papers. Just as she was telling me that in her shop, the *Shropshire Star* outsold the *Wrexham Leader,* someone came in to buy cigarettes. The newcomer now lived in the village, but had been born and brought up in a rural area of Denbighshire and was, she thought, only one of a handful of Welsh speakers in the area. I was still thinking about the woman who lived in Wales, but had to get a booster aerial to get decent reception for Welsh language television, when I boarded the bus for the last leg to Whitchurch.

Within minutes we had reached the border. I noticed that the Shropshire sign was smaller than the one now receding in the driver's mirror – the one that told drivers going the other way that they were entering Wales. The Welsh signs were always bigger – it was to be a pattern I would see many times as I moved between the countries. Why?

The Lancastrian editor of a glossy magazine, aimed at those who lived in a nearby English county, had offered an explanation.

'Because the border matters more to Wales than England.'

He also told me that 'people in north Wales can't understand those who live in the south.'

Really? It was news to me. Did he mean if they spoke in Welsh or English? He did not say, but I thought to him it did not matter; the sentiment was enough.

With variations, it was to be a phrase I was to hear on more than one occasion as I travelled between towns and villages on both sides of Offa's Dyke. But the only people who said it were English. I could never get to the core of what they meant – manners or circumstances prevented me from digging too far, yet by the time I had reached the end of my bus extravaganza, my overriding impression was that most of them were not talking about accents or dialects, but completely separate branches of the Welsh language. As Welsh speakers understand virtually everything they say to each other, why do 'outsiders' often say they can't? Divide and rule? Was I being thin-skinned again?

I might have had private reservations about the editor's reading of the linguistic map of Wales, but he dealt with some other, potentially complicated subjects, in brisk, forthright fashion. Within a few minutes, he had told me that 'borders still matter', 'borders *should* matter' and that he had never heard of 'border people.' Did they exist? I hoped that within the next month or two, I would find out and said so. After giving me a brief lecture on the history of Wales, he told me he liked the title of my book, and then wished me good luck. I was grateful for his insights and the time he had made in his busy day.

Shortly after leaving Hanmer, we arrived in Whitchurch. A book shop, just yards away from the bus station was to be my starting point. Within minutes, the thoughtful woman who worked there told me that 'Whitchurch is very *Shropshire'*. I had been to the town before and thought I knew what she meant. To me, an outsider, it did not appear to look towards anywhere in the outside world, but only in on itself. Wales could have been a country in South America for all the profile it had. Although the police force might be West Mercia and the Development Agency might be the West Midlands, it did not feel like a Midlands town to me, but nor did it appear to be a place where people travelled to the conurbations of the north-west for jobs or culture. It was not near any dominant city, and all the towns or big villages that surrounded it like numbers on a clock – like Market Drayton, Nantwich, Malpas, Wem, Ellesmere and Shrewsbury, seemed to exist in a type of geographical No Man's Land. It was in the middle of agricultural countryside, but it did not have the feel of a farming town. Even its name made understanding more difficult. If you look in a road atlas of the UK, you will find eight other towns or villages called Whitchurch, not counting Whitchurch Canicorum, Whitchurch Hill and Whitchurch-on-Thames. You will find them all over the southern half of Britain – from rural Pembrokeshire in the far west of Wales to Home Counties Buckinghamshire. You might find their name comes from 'White Church', and you might find it within you to understand my inability to place where it was. To me, it sounded like a made-up name, a bit like Borsetshire in the *Archers*, but it looked real enough as I talked to the nice woman in the book shop and asked her where she was from. Lancashire originally. Trying to place her, was very Welsh. She surprised me by using the same words that went through my mind.

'You sound very Welsh.'

She smiled; it was not an accusation, just a statement of fact.

'Do I?'

'Yes, we don't hear accents like that around here.'

'Do you get many people from Wales coming to Whitchurch?'

'Don't think so, but it's hard to tell if they come from just over the border ... as far as I know, they sound the same as people from around here.'

'So the border makes no difference?'

I was thinking about accents, but she was thinking more practically.

'Some people in the town would like your free prescriptions.'

It was my turn to smile, before asking another question, 'Maybe, but it wouldn't make them want to move to Wales would it?'

Her reply surprised me, 'Well, not just for free prescriptions, other things as well.'

'Such as?'

'You're going to have free car parking in hospitals, aren't you?'

'It looks like it, but things like that wouldn't make people move, would they?'

She nodded to emphasise the point before saying, 'Some people would swap countries for things like that.'

I was still thinking about what she had said as some new customers came into the shop. Could it be true?

The efficient, friendly woman spoke to the newcomers for a couple of minutes before they left and left us to carry on our conversation. We chatted about the possible referendum in Berwick-on-Tweed, and then she asked me why I was interested in borders. I told her about the book I was planning to write and asked more questions about Whitchurch. Our chat had the easy flow of decent tennis and, for the next few minutes we talked about the town. I learned that most people probably watched Midlands television and, thanks to a good rail connection, did their big shop in Shrewsbury. We moved on to perceptions, stereotypes and characteristics of people who live in other parts, while I listened and offered up a little prayer that I would meet more like her on my travels.

But I closed the door to the shop with an impression that her original description of the town seemed about right to me – Whitchurch was very Shropshire. Conversations I was to have in places like Shrewsbury and Clun reinforced the notion of Shropshire being almost a separate identity – a county with enough history to make at least some of those who lived within its boundaries feel Salopian first and English second.

It was time to look for a coffee shop so that I could sit down and think about what I had learned so far. If I had expected to find lots of 'Ye Olde Tea Shoppes', filled with chintz and waitresses wearing black dresses fringed with white collars and cuffs, I was going to be disappointed, but the coffee I drank in the café I chose, was good, strong and hot. Better still, no-one interrogated me about the type, strength, size of the drink I wanted. This was not Saturday night in Los Angeles or downtown New York – this was Whitchurch, Shropshire on a weekday afternoon.

In modern Britain, if you can speak coffee, you have arrived at Destination Cool. Someone who knows about espresso *ristresso* and *macchiato* is worth knowing. Someone who cruises the Derby Ring Road and chooses a *frappelatte* in the high heat of summer, is someone really worth knowing, as they will be amongst the coolest people in the whole of the East Midlands.

By the way, if you are ever talking to people who are fluent in coffee, it is as well to remember that they also say things like on–board, up–coming, left field, behind the eight ball and regular fries. They have even been known to use the word 'fall' instead of autumn. You have been warned. If you are prepared for this, you might be able to stop yourself from doing something you will regret later.

The usual suspects were up on the menu board, but thank goodness, no-one asked me to pronounce *macchiato*. I sipped an ordinary coffee, read a couple of local papers and thought about the time when I queued behind a mountainous fat woman in a Huddersfield café bar (yes, they do exist) and heard her ask for a 'skinny latte to go', while I reminded myself of a New Year resolution to be less judgemental in future. But I had not kept my resolution, because years later, here I was, still rushing to make judgements about a place I knew little about. Enigmatic Whitchurch deserved better.

A couple of hours and a number of conversations with helpful, friendly locals later, it was a man, newly determined to keep resolutions, but little wiser about broader and border issues, who strolled back to the bus station by the supermarket. I had plenty of time and I looked forward to finding a spot out of the cold wind that was beginning to spoil the day, settling down to finish my papers and eating the sandwich I had bought. When I found my place, a man with long unkempt hair, who was wearing layers of heavy old clothes, had beaten me to it. I was not surprised; he looked like a man who would be familiar with the hidden corners of most towns he visited.

'Come and sit down, there's plenty of room.'

A dirty hand patted the wall next to him, 'It's alright, I'm harmless.'

I must have looked a little doubtful or he must have got used to the effect he had on strangers, because he said reassuringly,

'Besides, you're bigger than me!'

He stood up to prove it and then attempted a smile through cracked lips. His smile was not a thing of beauty, but he was reassuringly small, so I sat next to him and raised a nicely neutral topic.

'Bit of a sharp wind.'

There was a brief silence while I did battle with the sandwich's cellophane straitjacket and he remembered some words. Within seconds, we were both successful.

'Daffodils that come before the swallow dares and braves the winds of March with beauty ... something like that anyway, good isn't it?'

He paused, and a quick, sly smile flitted over his stubbly face, 'Even though it's not quite March yet.'

'No, but it's good – Shakespeare?'

'Yes, the *Winter's Tale.*'

I suspected he was living rough, and suddenly, my ham salad sandwich lost its taste.

'Hungry?' His tired eyes brightened in anticipation.

'A bit ... '

'Do you want the other one?'

Five minutes later, I had been given his potted history. His teaching career had been cut short by something that had happened at a school in London. He had been renting a flat, but had to leave when his money ran out and I got the impression that his relationship with his parents had suffered. They had died within weeks of each other while he was on the road and he did not find out for months. He told the story with the detachment of a distant academic cousin digging around for clues to the life of a relative most of the family would rather forget.

'Where do you live?'

As a curious threadbare-looking dog peered around the corner, my new acquaintance smiled with a gentle acceptance of my conventional question and said, 'I don't really live anywhere, no that's not really true. I come to Whitchurch a lot, it's where I was brought up and sometimes I go down to London to a place for people like me.'

What do you say to a story like that? 'Oh ... ' was the best I could do.

'But it's not too bad.'

In my silence, he did more thinking. 'I don't miss much.'

'So you ... sort of travel about?'

'Yes.'

'Doesn't it get cold in winter?'

This time his smile was shy, not sly, 'Not with global warming!'

'Do you try and find out what's going on?'

'You mean the news?'

I nodded. 'Yes.'

'Oh I know what's going on, most days I read the papers.'

For a second or so he hesitated, and then gave me a quick, almost gleeful smile. 'People leave them lying around or just throw them away – they throw away lots of things that end up in my pockets!'

'Do you miss television?'

'I watch it in that place in London or in a pub if I've had a bit of luck, but I wouldn't care if I never saw it again.'

'Why?'

To the background noise of squabbling birds, he stopped touching his grimy face as he thought about an answer.

'When I watch it, I usually get angry … lots of things make me angry … lots of things.'

I asked him to give me some examples. This time there was no hesitation.

'Everyone knows what to say.'

'I don't understand.'

He began to walk around. 'Everyone knows what's expected of them – if something happens somewhere people always say this is a very close-knit community … '

He was building up a head of steam.

'I saw the start of a talent show the other night, *talentless* most of them were – they were all interviewed and said they *deserved* to be famous and they all had sob stories and some of the judges pretended to cry when the camera was on them and … '

He was beginning to scratch his face as he got angrier and I thought perhaps a change of subject might calm him down a bit.

'Do you travel up and down the border?'

The abrupt change of subject didn't appear to bother him, 'Which border?'

'The one between Wales and England.'

'Yes of course, and the one between England and Scotland. I've been all over, but borders don't matter to people like me.'

He hesitated. 'Not been to Ireland, though might do one day.'

'Are people the same everywhere?'

For a few seconds the man thought about the question. 'Don't think they are, I think they're worse in cities.'

'Wherever the city might be?'

'Yes, cities make us brutal.'

'It's a bit of a generalisation, but I think I agree.'

The man smiled, and pretended to be Noel Coward, 'Ah! Don't say you agree with me. When people agree with me I always feel that I must be wrong.'

Just before I showed my ignorance he said, 'Oscar Wilde … not sure which play … I used to know.'

The last few words were spoken in a sad summation of the way his life had gone. It was time for me to catch my bus and leave Whitchurch. Would he be insulted if I gave him some money?

'No, and thank you. Welsh people are very generous.'

He paused and said with a twinkle in those red-rimmed eyes, 'well … some of them are anyway and if you want some advice from me …'

'Well yes, of course.'

'Don't worry too much about making generalisations. Sometimes it's the only way to make sense of things.'

My bus was waiting and within minutes we were leaving the enigmatic town and heading towards a border that did not matter to the man with the red-rimmed eyes/

Oswestry to Llanfyllin

MANY OF THE LITTLE VILLAGES, found within the kick of a rugby ball from the north Shropshire town of Oswestry, sound as Welsh as *bara brith* or Tom Jones, and while places like Trefonen, Nantmawr and Hengoed might not have as many letters as Llanfairpwllgwyngyllgogerychwyrndrobwyllllantysiliogogogoch, they could still pass muster as the birthplaces of Welsh celebrities who love Wales so much they live somewhere else. We have all listened to these people trotting out polished anecdotes about their early lives when they appear on chat shows just before the launch of their latest something. We have all read about their childhoods in the pages of glossy magazines where pictures matter more than words. We know they grew up in villages where they sang in choirs, attended chapel and were kept awake at night by sheep coughing after days of breathing in fumes blown over their stunted grass from 'dark factories that scarred the land like a pox.'

By the way, any reader who fears the unexpected has no need to worry, because at some point the celebrity will undoubtedly say, 'everyone might have been poor, but it was a real community', in a voice which could have come from the bottom of the deepest pit in a valley that might have represented Wales in the Cultural Olympics. The journalist involved usually has the happy problem of wondering which clichés to choose for people who want the comfort of reassuring stereotypes. However, a lazy journalist, who has never been further west than Slough, might not realise until it was much too late, that all those little villages with those strange, difficult to pronounce names, are not in fact Welsh, but English. On the map at least, Oswestry is a Saxon island surrounded by a Celtic sea. Friends with local knowledge talk about Oswestry as an English border town where Welsh is spoken. They told me this time that the guide books were right; Oswestry was a part English, part Welsh mixture of a melting pot where Shropshire meets Wales, but somehow, I did not quite see it their way.

While preparing for my bus trip to Llanfyllin, I had a pleasant, informative conversation with three women who worked in a local Tourist Information Centre. Two told me they were English but really felt British, while the other, who was born in Wales, thought about things for a moment, and then said she was Welsh. We talked about accents – none of them could differentiate between the accents heard in and around Oswestry, how Shropshire has largely replaced Salop, county pride, their disappointment that the concept of Britain is slowly losing ground and the surprising fact that apparently lots of those who have moved to this part of Shropshire have chosen to give their houses names like *Cartref* or *Bryn Hafod*, even though they themselves had no Welsh connections.

Now, some three weeks later, and after days of heavy rain, the weather had perked up and it looked as if my trip would take place on a nice hot day. Heat meant thirst. Thirst meant water. With this logical sequence in mind, I set off to buy some. Although a family of Welsh speakers just beat me to the entrance of supermarket A, and there were bilingual signs in nearby supermarket B, I came outside into the sunshine still thinking Oswestry could have been a town miles away from the invisible line that separated the two countries. And so, just as noon was about to steal the good name of morning, I found an empty bench in the centre of Oswestry and sat down to look through the promotional material I had picked up at the Tourist Information Centre. Unlike some I was to see on my journey, the brochures and guides were well-written and mercifully free of too much gushing prose, although, as might be expected, there were dishonourable exceptions '… shadows of the past echo around this land of myth and legend' … 'Border fortifications resound with tales of a guarded landscape and the fear that shrouded the lives of its people …' As I was a connoisseur of this kind of stuff, I searched for more and found it over the page. 'Living on the edge can be to live among extremes, at times serene and tranquil, at other times dramatic and breathtaking. Water and land co-exist in an ever-changing scene, yet these stark contrasts bring their own beauty and invite us to explore.' Where was this? Where was the water? Was there a river or a beach somewhere? Had I missed them?

As locals bustled past me with plastic shopping bags full of everyday needs, I wondered if I should ask them if they enjoyed 'living on the edge', but then thought better of it; they had more useful things to do with their time than speak to a cynical visitor.

'Is this taken?'

A dumpy woman in her late fifties to be generous, gestured towards my rucksack on the bench next to me with hands where veins stood out like ranges of blue knobbly hills and ran south towards red knuckles. I moved the rucksack, smiled an apology and the woman sat down. She pointed towards the little pile of leaflets that lay between us, 'First time in Oswestry?'

'No, but it's the first time I've tried to look at it with the eyes of a stranger.'

'Why are you trying to do that?'

So I told her about my bus book and she told me about her life. As ever, I was amazed by the details some people give to a total stranger. She talked about her first and only husband. 'He was nice, but somehow we drifted apart, I think he had someone else … he said he didn't, but women know these things. He was always tired, he was too tired for bed if you know what I mean …'

I thought I did, but wished I did not.

'Do you have any children?'

'One, a boy. One was enough, he was huge and it was so painful, I was in labour for ... '

I tuned out as she started telling me the graphic details of waters breaking, and then attempted to ignore her words until she paused for breath. It was time to change the subject before she told me about the moment the baby was conceived.

'Are you from Oswestry?'

'No, I'm not sure where I'm from really ... I've moved all over, but I've lived around here for the past few years.

'In England?'

'No, just in Wales, but no-one takes much notice of the border. There's no need to really for things are more or less the same in Wales or England – except for health of course, but I've got a Welsh card, which is a bit of a saving.'

'What's a Welsh Card?'

'Well, my doctor's in Shropshire, but I live in Wales. We get free prescriptions. They send us a card through the post, like a credit card and if we take it to a chemist in Wales, we don't have to pay!'

'Don't most of the people who use the same surgery have to pay for their medicines?'

'Yes.'

'Do you think that's fair?'

She paused, and with the fingers of one hand, absent-mindedly stroked the blue hills on the back of the other while she thought of her answer.

'Probably not, but life's not fair is it?'

I walked through busy streets to the bus station and looked for someone to confirm the time of my return journey from Llanfyllin, but, as I was to find in most towns up and down the border, there was no-one to ask. Big laminated timetables were dotted around the place, but they only seemed to deal with outward journeys from Oswestry. Although I had drawn blank confusion in phone calls the day before, a trawl through a number of websites seemed to tell me that I would have the thick end of two hours in Llanfyllin before the trip back to Oswestry. If the sentence you have just read suggests that, for once at least, a travel website came up trumps, and was easy to use, forget it. A few days earlier, after much huffing and puffing, I found a West Midlands travel site, completed the 'Start' and 'Finish' boxes, and then waited for the results. But it was not as simple as that – it is *never* as simple as that. In order to find out the times of buses that ran between Oswestry and Llanfyllin, I had to supply the number of the service. How would I know the number? Only locals would know the number and they would know the times anyway! Do crazies run websites like this? But someone who would have the information at his fingertips, was behind the wheel of the Llanfyllin bus that pulled up a couple of minutes before departure time.

I waited my turn behind a little knot of fellow passengers and then asked the driver about return journeys.

'Not sure.' The question seemed to make him feel a little uncomfortable, 'but I'll have a look through these.'

For a few seconds, he riffled through a few individual route timetables before choosing one and running his finger down a column of figures.

'Ah ... just after half-past three, I think.'

I looked at the page he was holding. On the top was printed 'Llanfair Careinion.'

With a carefully neutral voice, I said, 'Is this the right one? I'm going to Llanfyllin.'

'Ah ... yes, of course.' His accent was south-east England.

He seemed anxious to be off; he had a timetable to follow.

'Are you driving this bus back?'

His answer was crisp and decisive. 'Yes, straight back.' This was a man on top of things.

'And you don't know if there's another one later?'

This time there was a hint of doubt. 'Don't think there is.'

And don't think I will be joining you for the journey, but thank you for your help. Sometimes sarcastic thoughts can be satisfying thoughts.

The next day, I caught an earlier bus and headed for Llanfyllin through the crowded streets of Oswestry. It only took a few moments for me to realise that the heating was on. It was quite a warm, sunny day, people were wearing light summer clothes, but the heating was on! I sat down, looked around, and wondered if I was having a middle-aged flush. The rich, mellow voice came from somewhere behind me. 'It'll be alright when we get going.' His accent was south Wales valleys. He pointed to the narrow opening at the top of the window, and then at the temporary traffic lights that were holding us up, 'Won't be long now ... as soon as we go, we'll get some air in through those.'

As the pitiless border sun (it's a bit of an exaggeration) tried to cook me through the glass, I turned and looked at the man and hoped he was right, because I was beginning to feel like a contestant on one of those Japanese TV programmes, where exhibitionists seeking fame and fortune have to endure extreme temperatures in a glass cube built on a tropical beach, whilst outside, everyone else splashes in the cooling sea or drinks cold beer from frosted cans.

'Shouldn't we ask the driver to turn the heating off?' All around me, people were busy ignoring my question.

The lights changed, but parked cars and oncoming vehicles meant cooler air remained a distant promise until we reached the outskirts of town and the original driver was replaced by Michael Schumacher. No-one, not even the little old ladies chatting away quite happily in the first few rows of seats, even twitched as we reached Mach 1 on a decent straight before having to decelerate for a village. Every time we slowed down near a little collection of houses, I could almost guarantee that someone in a garden would wave to someone they knew on the bus or one of my fellow travellers would interrupt a cheerful conversation to mime a greeting to a friend they could see through the windows that framed nostalgic scenes like a childhood memories.

Visitors to Britain should not expect this to be the norm. All over the country, millions of people never speak to those who live next door and in many a suburb, a brief nod to neighbour strangers has replaced the friendships of the past. But thinking about it, some of them might be strange neighbours ...

However the dark clouds of delinquent weather might, in the future, offer a silver lining. Why? Because although this might seem hard to believe for those who now live silent, insulated lives, in some towns there have been verified reports of neighbour strangers having brief conversations about the snowfall of the night before or the problems caused by hosepipe bans! I reckon it will only take about five more years of funny weather before we all become firm friends with people we currently ignore.

Within minutes I saw a Welsh flag on a tall pole in the back garden of a house and we passed the sign for the divided village of Llanymynech. It was one of those places you think you know but really do not, if you understand what I mean. However, one of the few things I felt reasonably confident about, was a belief that Caractacus made his last stand against the Romans from a defensive position on the top of Llanymynech Hill, just to the north-west of the village. If anyone is interested in such things, even a cursory study shows that while Iron Age hillforts can be found on craggy outcrops and hills all over the borderlands, the area around Oswestry seems to have more than its fair share. This knowledge brought back memories. I remembered that once, nearly twenty years ago, I had been asked to take thirty visiting American students to look at Old Oswestry, an iron-age fortress, just north of the town, that was probably first occupied about 300 BC. The afternoon before we went, I had told them where we would be going the next day. They had listened and then started leaping up and down with joy. A real life fortress! Tribal conflict! Ramparts! Ditches! Battles! They had seen it in films and now they were going to see it in real life! I do believe most of them hardly slept with the sheer excitement of it all. Intermittent early morning rain had not dampened their spirits and it had been a cheerful group of students and one apprehensive Welshman who had boarded the bus in Wrexham for the short trip to the fortress. Had I given them false expectations? I had told them they would have to use their imagination here and there, but had they believed me? As we neared the site, the driver had asked me when he should come back to pick us up. I glanced through the windows and did some thinking. The rain seemed to have stopped for a while at least.

'About half twelve.'

That would give us a couple of hours. I did not know at the time it was going to feel much longer than that. In the days before mobile phones, the driver had left for Oswestry and breakfast. Even before the bus was out of sight, there seemed to be more moisture in the air and I began to think that two hours was going to be plenty long enough. Some of the students had asked me when we would get our first glimpse of the fort. Would they be able to see it in the far distance from the top of the hill over there? *It is actually on top of the hill over there, you are looking at it now, but I cannot tell you that, perhaps you will think it is more impressive up close.* I tried a brave smile. 'Be patient, soon all will be revealed!'

A few minutes later, they were on the hill looking at the fort's defences. It has to be said that there are probably more dramatic sights in the world than the few grass-covered concentric ditches and ramparts that surround the plateau where settlers had built their simple round huts. The students, fresh in from the sunshine of an American summer, had stood around under dark British skies and looked puzzled. It then began to rain and within seconds the students were standing around under dark British skies looking puzzled *and* damp.

'Where are the huts?'

It was a pity the girl who had asked the question wore an anorak that did not have a hood. I tried to bring a smile to her shiny wet face.

'Nothing lasts forever!' The attempt had failed, as did my almost manic efforts to paint word pictures of what the fort might have been like all those years ago and it had been an increasingly drenched, sullen and resentful bunch of students who trailed behind me as we headed back to the pick-up point. Just as I thought that Hollywood had a lot to answer for, the coach had arrived a blessed ten minutes early. It cannot be said that the visit had been quite the success my boss had hoped for when he included it in his plans for an 'exciting and informative orientation week.' But back to Llanymynech.

In the years when some parts of Wales were 'dry' on Sundays, I had read about a pub which straddled the border, where drinkers could be served in one of its two 'English' bars, but not in the 'Welsh' one on the west side of the building. More recently I had been told me about the local golf club where some holes were in England and some in Wales and I wondered if there were many courses in the world where you could hit a ball as far as another country. I did not know if the story is factually correct, but it put a little smile on my face when I heard it.

I had also heard about a Welsh-speaking Welshman who lived in the part of the village that lay in Wales, who was in a running dispute with the post office sorting depot in Shrewsbury over his address. Although he had the 'SY' of a Shrewsbury post code, he wanted a 'Welsh' address. Does it matter? Yes, if you have strong beliefs. Most things matter if you have strong beliefs. As we passed fields of grass the colour of winter cabbage, and another flagpole – this one with the Welsh dragon above the cross of St George, I carried on a sporadic conversation with the man with the baritone voice. He lived near the village of Llansantffraid-ym-Mechain, which must have presented pronunciation problems for at least some of the Scousers who had moved there in recent years.

I was surprised by the news. 'Are there many?

'Enough for a little place like this.'

Enough said. Within minutes he wished me well, then got off the bus and waved goodbye as we got underway.

Another man, this one with kind, tired eyes, who must have been listening from his seat across the aisle, took up the baton of conversation about Scousers. As we spoke, a frown replaced what I thought would be his normally good humoured expression.

'They've been settling here for years.'

'But why Liverpool?'

'Football probably.'

'What do you mean?'

For the next few minutes I was told about the complicated recent history of what used to be a village football team. The story was based on change. As the team moved up through the leagues, most local players who had once played for nothing or beer money, had been replaced by outsiders, many from Liverpool, who were attracted by the relatively good wages on offer thanks to sponsorship from commercial companies. Change was not confined to playing personnel. The team changed its name from Llansantffraid to Total Network Solutions, and then had morphed into The New Saints. Success in the semi-pro Welsh Premier League meant an entry to the second tier European football competition – the UEFA Cup – and trips to distant parts of Europe. Listening to him brought back an item I had once heard on the regional news. A couple of die-hard fans from a tiny village in Powys had driven an old van thousands of miles across Europe to somewhere near the Caucasus mountains so that they could watch whatever their football team was called at the time, play *F.C. Utterli Unpronounsabl*. The supporters got back half-way through the cricket season, but said in an interview, the trip had been worthwhile. Make up your own minds.

The changes did not stop there. These days, although they are still in the

Welsh Premier League, The New Saints do not even play in Wales, but across the border in Oswestry. The story reminded me of one of those sixties pop groups who, because of legal disputes between the founders, still tour under a slightly different name, have only one remaining original member (usually an ancient drummer with wispy hair and a face that looks like a walnut), but still play the only two hits anyone can remember. My informative friend ended the conversation with an update on recent developments. A new village team had been formed with *local* players and things were going well. I hoped their success would continue; mercenaries are never attractive. His timing was immaculate, because he completed the story just as we reached his stop.

I half listened to scraps of conversations as we crossed a pleasing stone bridge that arced high above the river Cain that flowed within its rocky banks and I tried but failed to remember the surname of someone from Llanfyllin I had known in my distant student days. Maybe it was the heat.

An elderly couple negotiated a drop-off point with an obliging driver as we drove along a road that ran through what looked like rich pasture land to a townie like me. Within a few hundred yards, an agricultural smell wafted through the bus and we heard a middle-aged woman tell the friend sitting next to her she 'should have waited till she got home!' Both were still laughing as we swept around a corner and reached our destination.

I have been calling Llanfyllin a village, but I was wrong; it might have only some 1200 people, yet it had been a town for over 700 years. Dark clouds had begun to shade the battle with morning sun as I headed towards St Myllin's, the church one local historian had said was 'the heart of Llanfyllin.' On the way, I passed a restaurant with a name that ended in an 's' and wondered if there were any places where the final 's' is unknown. I had my doubts, because for more than a decade, the country had been sinking under a tidal wave of restaurants, clubs, cafés, bistros and tea rooms called things like Greens, Rules, Judges, Staggers and Shaggers. Stan, a friend of mine who knows these things, once told me that in a couple of towns, adding an 's' is a condition for planning permission, but I was not convinced. More research was needed.

Across the quiet road, I saw an old farmer, wearing faded bib overalls and a flat cap, stand and glance down at his mobile phone while, at his side, a docile dog looked up at his master's lined and weathered face. For a few seconds I wondered if the sight might be a metaphor for something profound, but was not profound enough to think of it.

I had not done much research before the trip so the size of the church came as a surprise. It was a big, imposing building surrounded by well-tended grounds. Inside, I found a whole range of booklets that suggested that St Myllins still had a role to play in the community, even in these days of text messages and televised celebrity pig racing on ice. There was some interesting stuff dotted around these well-written pages and so I stood inside the lighted church and learned a little about the life and times of St Myllins and its town. Hard facts might have been in short supply, but there were enough to suggest that the church, or its predecessors, had been around for over 1400 years and had a rich history to match. As half a dozen smiling ladies of a certain age passed me and walked towards a meeting room, I read about one comparatively recent episode.

In 1812, following a bloody battle in the Peninsular Wars, a young French officer, together with some 150 of his compatriots, was captured, placed on parole, and sent to Llanfyllin. Lieutenant Pierre Augeraud, described as being tall, with blue eyes, brown hair and a fresh complexion, was billeted opposite the church in the big 'Council House'. Apparently he spent hours painting murals (they still exist) in his billet and looking through an upstairs window in the hope of catching a glimpse of young Mary Williams, the daughter of the rector, William Williams. The booklet did not say where and when Mary succumbed to his devilish Gallic charm, but in 1813, her dying father arranged to put a stop to this nonsense and the young officer was sent back to France under the terms of a prisoner exchange. By 1815, the war might have been over, but conflict still raged in the mind of a Llanfyllin woman. Would the young Frenchman return as promised? I read on, absorbed by a romance now nearly two hundred years old: 'There's a knock at the door. Mary doesn't look up from her sewing: she has been disappointed too many times. A shadow falls across her …' Yes it was Pierre, proving that sometimes even a man can keep a promise made in a moment of passion.

In the quiet of a late morning, I left St Myllins, crossed the road and looked for somewhere to eat. I could ask a local, but it would not be the thin man with wispy blond hair who was hanging around near a public toilet. He might have been innocently waiting for a friend, but he was not going to make a new one in me. Loitering is such a descriptive word. Walking back to the centre of town, enjoying the gentle breeze on my face, I passed a pub and saw, next to the front door, a plaque which read 'Bert Davies Memorial Ramp.' Sure enough, a gently sloping concrete runway would make it easier for wheelchair users to get inside and have a drink. Was Bert a regular? Was Bert disabled? Was Bert the chief fundraiser? I walked on, feeling, for some inexplicable reason, much better about life, the universe and all that.

A café on the main street seemed as good a place as any and within minutes I was sitting down, eating my lunch-time snack, half listening to the easy-going conversations that flowed around me in accents ranging from Eastenders to the Archers. Three white-faced girls, all dressed in black with hair the colour of a *Mafiosi's* coat, came in and, as they waited for their coffees, bitched about an absent friend. Listening to them, I wondered how they would speak about someone they *really* did not like and what it must be like growing up in and around a small town in mid Wales. Before my visit I had looked at the results of a survey about local teenagers and found that apparently nearly 50 % of those questioned described themselves as being Plastics, Emos, Greebos, Sporties or Goths. Dredging up my miniscule stock of knowledge on such matters, I decided the girls were probably Goths, but as I had no idea what a Plastic, Emo or Greebo looked like, my guess was probably way off the mark.

What did I think about Llanfyllin? I opened a notebook and tried to assemble some random thoughts. I was sitting in a café offering Tuna Melts to customers living in or passing through a tiny town, miles from the sea, where nearly 40% of the population spoke an ancient language – Welsh. Lots of varied events were held in the area, including a thriving summer Workhouse Festival and spring concerts featuring the likes of the Allegri string quartet, so perhaps, on this occasion at least, the purple prose about a town bursting with creativity and culture, might have been based on something approaching reality.

Despite being miles away from the big, bad city, local teenagers could identify with the latest fashion, music and ways of talking to each other because these days, there were no walls around the town to keep them out.

I sort of told him like he had gone too far, but he was like ... angry you know?

Yeah ... but his dad was like ... nearly home so it was like time to. go, I was soooo not happy ...

History should record that these words were written by someone who left youth culture behind many, many years ago and thought that an Emo was a flightless bird. Don't groan.

To me, a casual visitor, Llanfyllin didn't have the feel of being a particularly

'Welsh' town. The Essex speakers in the corner might have had something to do with this, but other, more subtle reasons were involved. Was it the local accent? Perhaps. Here harsh edges had been smoothed off by centuries of living in an accessible valley bordering a much bigger neighbour with an all pervasive culture. The girl Goths might have had hard views but they spoke in soft accents. I thought some more, wrote 'Plastics live in an ancient town built from traditional materials' then looked up in time to see a youngish woman with short, prematurely grey hair, come into the café and order a decaffeinated coffee. I had never seen her in my life before, but that did not stop me from jumping to a series of linked conclusions...

- She lived locally, but had been born in London or somewhere in the south-east.
- Her parents had money.
- She had been to a private school and a good university.
- She had moved to Llanfyllin ten years ago to enjoy a 'better quality of life.'
- She belonged to an artistic group called something like Red Square or Blue Moon which
received public money for running festivals and 'inclusive, innovative projects.'
- Her children were called Alfie, Phoebe, Lettie and Bertie.
- She was once married to a city financier, but now lives with a painter called Joss.
- They wanted to have their own baby who would be given a spiritual Celtic name ...

The community artist pulled a big writing pad made from recycled paper (it would have to be) from a dun-coloured cloth bag slung across her shoulder, frowned, then started making notes. I watched and wondered what was troubling her. As tiny worry lines deepened on her pert, heart-shaped face, I suddenly knew the questions she needed to answer. Should the festival have an opening event or should it just happen? Starting to the right of Organic Options, should it be Healing Zone, Earth Yurt, Kids' Play *then* Clowning for Health, or would Lizzie be annoyed because she was *always* next to Tim?

At the time, I did not know that in the months to come, I would be meeting her sisters in pleasant little towns up and down the border between England

and Wales – hundreds of them. Was anyone left living in Surrey? A boy and a girl, both in their mid-teens, looked into the café as if they were early for a meeting with friends. They hovered undecided, then walked across the road. He was very thin. She was like a little pear. Both had raggedly cut fringes that swept over one eye. Streaks of pink in their hair stood out like acid lightning. Both wore very tight black tee- shirts covered with images of shaggy-haired guitarists and jeans which could only be removed through a surgeon's skill. As they walked away, I noticed their belts. His was like an endless chess board, all black and white checks while hers was studded and looped around fleshy hips and bottom and I wondered if they were telling the world that not every young person growing up in small, rural towns and villages wanted to drive tractors or knit woollen jumpers for plump women who could deliver a lamb before breakfast.

Outside, the afternoon was beginning to close in as clouds darkened the soft green hills that surrounded Llanfyllin. Plenty of time before the bus; it was time to sit and think about the trip so far.

'Mind if I sit down?'

The deep voice came from a big man about my own age who looked as if he spent most of his day working outdoors. His face was tanned, his hands were scarred and calloused and I knew that a strong body had come from hours doing hard manual work rather than circuits in a gym where people dressed in the latest designer kit and wiped away tiny beads of sweat with perfumed wrist bands. I moved my rucksack, gestured to the bench beside me and said, 'Sorry.'

'Don't worry, no need to apologise, we're always doing it.'

'What?'

'Apologising.'

He shook his head, smiled, then carried on, 'someone steps on our foot and what do we do?'

'We say sorry.'

The two middle-aged men on a bench chortled, whatever a chortle sounds like, I am not sure anyone knows.

Within minutes I knew quite a lot about the man next to me. He was from Cardiff originally, but had spent most of his life as an agricultural contractor. His work had taken him around the country – from Lincolnshire to Suffolk, before he ended up back in south Wales.

What was he doing in Llanfyllin?

'Visiting old friends. We come up every few months.'

'Do you like it round here?'

'Yes, it's OK. They seem to enjoy it anyway, lived here for years but ...'

He paused for a few seconds as a passing noisy lorry gave him time to think, and then carried on in a slightly hesitant way, 'but it might be one of those places where outsiders are never really accepted, they're just tolerated.'

I thought back to the Essex speakers in the café. 'By outsiders, do you mean English people?'

'Yes and no ... I suppose I mean that locals might not always like each other, but at least they generally look at the world in the same way.'

It was my turn to hesitate, 'So if you were born far away ...'

'There's less chance of seeing things the same ... yes, got to be right, hasn't it?'

For a few seconds, we looked across the road at an attractive young couple pushing an expensive buggy with matching child while I wondered how I should phrase my next question.

'You've knocked about a bit.'

He broke in and spoke quickly as he repeated the words. 'You've knocked about a bit ... sounds like a tongue twister ... whatever happened to them?'

'She sells sea shells on the sea shore.'

'Red lorry yellow lorry red lorry yellow lorry red ...'

The man from Cardiff suddenly shouted, 'Faster!' before I got in a tangle and thought that being born around the same time might help give a similar perception of the world. After a few seconds, I asked him if English and Welsh people looked at things in the same way.

'Well ...' This was a thoughtful man.

'I know it's difficult to generalise but ...'

He gave the question more thought, then me an answer.

'Don't think they do.'

'What do you mean?'

'Well, I know they're not all the same, but I've noticed a lot of English people feel happier organising things rather than letting things happen.'

'Is that good or bad?'

'Neither, depends on the circumstances. Some things have to be organised, but ...'

'But what?'

He shrugged. 'They enjoy running things, I suppose.'

'And we don't?'

The man from Cardiff gave the question more consideration. 'Some of us do, but most keep their head down and just do as they're told.'

'Why?'

'People are different. Maybe it's in our nature or something.'

'Maybe.'

While I wondered if he was right, he asked what I was doing in Llanfyllin. In less than thirty seconds I had given him what was becoming a well-practised reply.

'Surely you can't write about a place you've only been to for five minutes!'

I smiled apologetically, 'I'm afraid I can and do. It's not meant to be a guide book or anything so ...'

'So you told me, but you can't make your mind up about a place until you've lived there, can you?'

It was my turn to go on the attack. I loved little disagreements like these; they added a touch of spice to the day.

'Didn't you just tell me Llanfyllin was OK?'

He paused, sensing danger, before saying warily, 'Well, I think it is.'

'But you've never lived here, have you?'

'No but ...'

'And yet you gave me an opinion about the place. You told me what sort of town you thought it was.'

'I suppose I did, nothing wrong with that, is there?'

'Course not, we all do it all the time.'

He smiled. 'I see what you mean.'

I smiled back. 'The only difference with me is that I happen to be writing it down, probably a waste of effort anyway.'

'Why do you say that?'

'Because I doubt if anyone would want to publish a book like this. It's not a sexy subject is it? Besides, I'm not a writer.'

'Aren't you?'

'I do a bit of freelance writing, but I've never had a book published.'

He said, 'Well let's hope someone publishes Offa', while I thought how lucky I had been to have this conversation with a nice-natured man. Maybe it would bring me the luck I would need to persuade someone to publish the book.

For a few moments we talked about other books, films, food and rugby, quickly followed by growing up in south Wales and recent changes to Cardiff (most of them good) and Swansea (most of them bad). I enjoyed the conversation with the man from my own part of the world.

'So you'll carry on until you reach the Severn ...'

'Or someone smacks me for writing nasty things about their little bit of the country.' I hoped his smile was not one of anticipation. The bus came into sight, stopped to disgorge its passengers, before moving off to turn around. It was time to go.

'Best wishes, you might need them!'

We shook hands like old friends before I crossed the quiet road to wait for the bus to take me back to Oswestry. Two teenagers sat on some steps and carried on a desultory conversation about 'A' levels while I half listened and wondered if they would return to Llanfyllin after university. As we waited, dancing dust swooped and hovered before us in an unexpected burst of sunshine air and I tried to answer the age old question – what is another word for synonym? Travellers take note – taking buses on a regular basis can produce some strange side effects.

On the journey back, I thought about the day. Despite my initial misgivings, Oswestry was probably the most 'border' town I had been to on my travels so far, some way ahead of Wrexham and Chester. An hour spent wandering around Oswestry, talking to locals and reading a local paper might tell a stranger they were at least near another country – Wales. It was difficult to 'place' Llanfyllin. It did not feel like a border town, a particularly Welsh town or a little town in the Home Counties, it was something else again. Perhaps understanding would come later.

As we pulled into Oswestry bus station, I began to realise the limitations of my research technique. Getting to grips with cities, towns, villages or three-house hamlets can sometimes take years, yet I was trying to do it in hours and days. Perhaps I needed to consider a different approach. I considered it all the way down the aisle and then reached the decision that it was too late to change. Next stop, Montgomery.

Montgomery to Shrewsbury

IN THE GREY QUIET of an early May morning, as tiny showers of fine rain blurred the outline of roofs and rocks, I drove towards Montgomery and wondered if it had changed since I had last visited the little town that had given its name to one of the counties of Wales. My memories might have been positive, but were faded through the passing of years I could never get back. It was not fair, but nor is life which teaches us that you have got to get on with things while you can, including the first bus to Shrewsbury which was due to arrive any time soon. Easy. Well, it should have been, but for some reason timetables, common sense and the man who wrote these words, far from being the three *amigos*, usually turn out to be complete strangers.

My research had suggested that the Shrewsbury bus would leave from in front of the town hall in the main square, aka Broad Street, but unfortunately it did not tell me about the tiny fair being put in position as I arrived. Only a bike could get between the waltzers and roundabouts; a bus, even a small country bus, would have to take a different route. But a local would be able to tell me the routine, so, as the minutes ticked away, I found somewhere to park and then looked around for a suitable candidate. Within yards of the post office, I found one in a man with the weathered face of someone who had spent a working lifetime in fresh air, sunshine and howling gales.

'Morning.'

He smiled, nodded a greeting and replied, 'Morning.' Having established friendly relations, it was time to ask a question.

'I want to get a bus to Shrewsbury so ...'

'Won't come in here,' the man gestured towards the rides, 'won't be able to get in.'

'No, I was wondering where it'll go from.'

He pointed towards the main road, now temporarily hidden behind brightly painted machinery, 'Over there, I'll just check though.'

To me at least his accent seemed impressively local and locals know these things, but despite these reassuring feelings, the odd doubt still hung around as I followed him over to a somewhat younger man, setting up a market stall. My local friend pointed in my direction.

'He's going to Shrewsbury, by *bus*.'

The trader paused for a minute while he thought about the news.

'Won't get in here.'

'I told him that.'

My local laughed while the trader pointed to a spot beyond a roundabout.

'Goes from over there, you'd better hurry, it'll be here soon.'

I glanced down at my erratic watch and wondered how many minutes fast it was. It was usually ahead of its time, but if I was going to catch buses up and down the border, perhaps it would be better to set it as accurately as possible. But it was too late now.

'Quick, it's there.' My old friend was spot on. 'It'll go down the road, turn, and then come back through.'

Part of the bus could just be seen behind a waltzer and so I thanked him and rushed over to catch it. Judging by the quick glance I had while narrowly avoiding an oncoming car, the bus was going to Welshpool, but I was probably wrong. It must have just come *from* Welshpool. Soon the friendly driver would change the sign … yes that would be it. You are ahead of me now. I hopped aboard and immediately the bus started off down the hill. It already carried a few passengers who sat talking quietly as we reached the outskirts of the little town before turning and heading back towards the centre.

A few minutes later, I realised we seemed to have missed the turn to Shrewsbury. For a second or two, I considered getting off, but then rejected the idea. After all, this rural bus must be going somewhere in and around the border, so I might as well sit tight and wait. As we drove along roads that meandered up and down soft green hills and through well-cared for villages, I tried to work out where we were, but luckily, in less than a mile, a signpost told me we were probably heading for Welshpool. The destination on the front of the bus had been correct after all; the mistake had been mine. Subsequent enquiries told me the Shrewsbury bus was timetabled to leave a few minutes after the one I caught. Finding that out before the trip might have been a good idea.

Most places change, if only superficially, and Welshpool, a town I had first visited many years before, was no exception. After confirming the time of the next Shrewsbury bus with our friendly and helpful driver, I walked away to see what those changes might be, but first it was time for a bacon sandwich. The middle-aged woman who served me spoke with what I took to be a local accent so I asked her if Welshpool was a 'Welsh' town. Her answer gave me one interpretation of my question, although I had meant another.

'I suppose it depends which day of the week you're talking about – on market days, farmers come down from the hills and speak Welsh.'

'Are you Welsh?'

'Well I was born in Wales but I canna speak Welsh.'

I tried another question. 'Can't you be Welsh even if you don't speak the language?'

The woman thought about for a moment and then said, 'Yes of course, but you probably *feel* more Welsh if you can speak it … do you want brown sauce?'

My sandwich had arrived.

The town seemed to have grown since I was last here, but maybe I had shrunk; you do when you get older. Although there were signs of the recession, including shops for sale, discounted goods and a couple of empty offices, Welshpool seemed to be doing as well as might be expected. There was something else as well. It might have its share of places where you could buy paesan paninis and triple waffle burgers with regular fries, but as befits its name, Welshpool still seemed to be in Wales. The people I spoke to were courteous and helpful, the Shrewsbury bus would be along soon. I had enjoyed the sandwich – things were looking up.

A few months earlier, while doing some freelance work, I had come across a brief article written in 1877 for *Bye-Gones*, a weekly magazine aimed at those living in Wales and the Border Counties. The correspondent, who signed himself or herself 'R.E.D.', declared that there were now 'no fewer than eight variations of the pronunciation of Shrewsbury', then listed them before adding a few comments on some of the variants.

Apparently R.E.D thought that while Showsbury or Srowsbury was a semi-refined pronunciation, pronouncing the town as Shrowsbury showed someone to be 'classical and educated'. In the opinion of the writer at least, the use of Sosebury in country areas was preferable to Srewsbury, Shewsbury and the 'utterly vulgar Sewsbury'. I had made that seven, not eight, but perhaps I was forgetting about Shrewsbury itself – it had all got a little confusing, but however it was pronounced, I was on my way to the county town that had grown up in the loop of one of our great rivers – the Severn, where I was to finish my journey.

Just over half-way to Shrewsbury, a whine came from somewhere towards the back of the bus. It wasn't the engine; it was what turned out to be a skinny pale-faced teenager using a mobile phone to ask a girl to look for something ... Samantha, it's important ... really important. The whine continued all the way to the bus station. Those wanting more details can either skip forward to the Presteigne – Leominster chapter, or use their own imagination to decide what he had asked Sam to find ... if we're ever told ...

A decade ago, other passengers would have asked him to be quiet. In my father's time he would have been facing an operation to have the phone surgically removed. Now, no-one could touch him, except the police, provided they had been given written permission by the Home Office Minister for Expense Accounts. Things change. These days, he would know his rights, but not his responsibilities.

The countryside we were passing through was not dramatic, but it was pretty and peaceful. Glimpses gave interest; two old caravans at the bottom of a sloping field, a couple of donkeys, a lone black-faced sheep, a distant flock of circling birds and sunshine that rippled across the grass when breaks in the clouds allowed it to escape and touch the land I could see through the windows. In a few minutes, we reached the hospital stop on the western outskirts of Shrewsbury, before wending our way through what seemed to be a fairly recently built suburb until we joined a road flanked by comfortable older houses where owners were listening to Radio Four and rolling out their home-made pasta while dogs called Freud waited to be taken for a walk. Soon we were on the last lap heading down towards Frankwell, the Welsh Bridge and the bus station, listening to the last whining pleas of a teenager whose voice made fingernails scraping down a blackboard sound pretty damn good.

Fifteen minutes later, I was standing on the English Bridge, writing notes and staring at a river which was broader than I remembered, when a very neat, precise man, with glasses bigger than Deirdre Barlow's, wearing a checked shirt, soft-green woollen tie, fawn trousers and a grim jacket the colour of French mustard, told me that Shrewsbury was once the 'Capital of the Marches'. He had been walking past, saw my rucksack and thought I was a tourist who needed help, or so he said, but afterwards I wondered if he just spent his days circling the town, looking for people who did not know him.

Within seconds he was in full flow, his brow furrowed as he struggled to choose the right words to use. He spoke in a halting way, with random emphases here and there, that just stopped short of being a speech impediment. With a look of pained concentration on his slender pale face, he said, 'In this ... *context*, the word 'March' means a ... a ... *frontier* ... yes that's perhaps the best way I could ... *describe* it to someone like you.'

He had recognised my limitations. I was just starting to thank him for his tolerance, when he suggested we should get out of the rain that was beginning to plaster his sparse fair hair. He must have sensed my hesitation, because he added a clincher.

'They call me ... *Barry.*'

It was my turn to frown – they call me Barry? Was it his real name or a title? Was I speaking to the Supreme Leader of a dubious cult? But the man they called Barry might give me the wit and wisdom I needed and besides which, he would probably know more about Shrewsbury than anyone on earth. So, in less than the time it took him to tell me that he had always been severely gifted, we were sitting down drinking cups of tea in what I took to be a vegetarian café, where, judging by the rich aroma that greeted us, the day's specials included 'very boiled sprouts'. As other customers chatted or read books and broadsheets, I asked Barry if he had been born and brought up in the town. For some reason, the question seemed to give him more trouble than

I thought it would. His frown lines deepened as he thought about an answer. What a difficult question to begin with! Then finally, after a few false starts, he spoke.

'I ... wasn't actually *born* here ... not in the sense you mean.'

It was my turn to look puzzled, but I did not say anything and sat there waiting for Barry to answer the complex question in his own way.

'This is ... *difficult* ... technically I was born in Shropshire.' He smiled. 'I always try to be precise.'

'Were you brought up in Shrewsbury?'

Barry considered the question as a woman carrying a dark green file joined a chubby man sitting at the next table. I had noticed him when we came in. He was eating something good for you with a fork held in his meaty right hand, while the other manipulated a newspaper with the skill of a conjurer.

'I've ... *lived* here, yes.'

'For long?'

The man they call Barry gave this difficult request for more information a few moments' thought. I expected his answer to contain some precision, but I was to be surprised.

'Long enough to understand.'

What did he mean? Should I ask him? I looked again at his pale, frowning, tense face but thought I could not heap more pressure on a man who was at the cutting edge of precise answers.

It was time to tell him I was planning to write a book. After I had trotted out my usual explanation, Barry surprised me by stating that he had, 'Welsh connections.'

'But you're not Welsh?'

'Not ... no not as you might ... shall I say, *understand* it.'

I paused while I thought that pursuing that line might take me past retirement age, so I asked a simpler question— one based on something I had read in some of the town's promotional brochures.

'Do you think of Shrewsbury as the 'gateway to Wales?'

'Yes and ... no.'

By this time I had realised that, wherever possible, the best strategy might be to say nothing and let Barry guide me through some complicated issues.

'Yes ... it is on a ... *natural* communications route into Wales, he hesitated while the faintest of smiles reached his thin, almost bloodless lips, 'think *roads*

... think *river* ... the Severn rises in Plynlimon ... think *travel*.'

He stopped speaking for a moment, and then gave me a smile that this time touched his eyes. 'But didn't you say, *the* gateway to Wales?'

I nodded. 'Yes, that's what I said.'

'So I couldn't agree with the ... shall I call it ... *description*, because there are other gateways to Wales ... Chester, Leominster, Ludlow, Chepstow, English towns that ...'

It was time to break in. 'But Chepstow's in Wales!'

His face told me he disagreed. 'At present it is, *technically* anyway, but some people think it should be in England.'

'Who?'

'Well, English Democrats, for a start.'

'Don't know much about them.'

He leant back in his chair and while I sipped my weak and weary tea, told me all about English Democrats and their plans for parts of my country. Apparently, the Party is organised on the basis of administrative areas which includes 'South West England.' In the list of counties you might expect to see under this title – Devon, Somerset and the like was ... Monmouthshire! Yes that's right – the Monmouthshire that most of us think is in Wales, the same Monmouthshire that gave the rugby world the Pontypool front row. I needed a strong drink, but another cup of tea would have to do for now.

As more people came in for lunch, Barry launched into details about the English Democrat's *Welsh* Assembly Election campaign in 2007. Was he serious? He was. Later I did some checking and found that the party had indeed fielded a couple of candidates in south-east Wales and gained *c*. 0.2% of the vote. Was he a member of English Democrats? Apparently not, or so he said, but I was beginning to suspect that deep within this man's mind, truth and fantasy were a little frayed around the edges. Somehow I dragged him back to Shrewsbury – had the town ever been Welsh? There was a brief pause while he considered the matter. 'It was *captured* I suppose you'd say, by Llewellyn, but was then taken back.'

'When was this?'

This time there was no hesitation or furrowed brow. Barry was on a roll.

'1215 ... look, recently I read something on a message board that you might not like but does *represent* one point of view.'

He looked across at me. 'Ready?'

'Go on … as my father used to say, I'm all ears … none of us are perfect.'

Barry did not smile. He would not, but I did when I thought of my father. Like most of us he had his stock of phrases to meet most occasions, including the one I have just written. But then my brief moment of happiness disappeared as I wished he was still alive, although I am not sure what he would have done if he had been around to hear Barry say, 'Wales has never been a country as such – just *that little bit on the left.*'

The last six words were in quotation marks written in the air by two fingers on each hand. Showing my new found maturity, I glanced at my watch like a mime artist, frowned and then stood up.

'I'm afraid I going to have to go, things to do and buses to catch.'

His eyes narrowed as he digested the news.

'Are you … *sure*? I haven't told you … how Powys was once … shall we say, *big* enough to reach the Midlands and we haven't even talked about Pengwern or south Rhedeg!'

'South Rhedeg', I shook my head, opened my hands in a gesture of disappointment and said, 'what a pity, but no time this time. Thanks for your information.'

I nodded my appreciation. 'It's been very helpful.'

We shook hands and I left. When, outside, I turned to wave, I saw he was already looking at a menu. I walked through the streets searching for somewhere to buy a watch battery, thinking about the man they call Barry and hoping the special was still available. A few minutes later, I was the only customer in a jeweller's shop speaking to a tall and very thin assistant who assured me the new battery should mean no more problems. I glanced around at the items on display and decided to ask a question.

'When you're out, do you always look at people's watches?'

'What do you mean?'

His tone was curt, his face could have been taken from an Easter Island statue and I wished I had just paid, thanked him and gone; but now I had started, I had to finish.

'I just wondered if you're out somewhere, you know in the pub with your friends, do you look at everyone's watches – occupational hazard, professional interest and all that.'

While I was babbling like a fool, I stared at the man and thought that if he had many friends, I still had a chance of playing rugby for Wales.

'No', he pointed to the door behind me, 'when I close that, I go home and don't think about watches until I open it again in the morning.'

Should I try and get him onto subjects like borders, perceptions, devolution and the like? What do you think? You are right; I just paid him and left.

For the next hour I wandered around the streets of the town and looked for signs that it was 'the Gateway to Wales.' As usual, the exercise yielded a disjointed series of impressions. In the window of a sports shop, I saw one red training top with a familiar three-feather logo. Not far away, outside a café, I saw an A-frame board advertising the coffee served inside. The coffee was Welsh (or ground and blended in Wales or whatever) and the message bilingual. Near a truly dreadful piece of modern sculpture that added nothing to the charm of this medieval town which, according to the guide books, had more than 600 listed buildings, I was sitting, wondering if I was hungry when I heard valley voices belonging to a cheerful convoy of smiling men and women heading towards Pride Hill.

The Visitor Information Centre in black and white Rowley's House was filled with Japanese tourists and French exchange students sent out to fill in fact sheets and learn something about the town. The staff seemed knowledgeable and tolerant and the material I collected was, in the main, free from the gushing prose of some I had collected on my trip so far. Restraint is always better than being bashed over the head by hyperbole.

As the names of roads are sometimes useful clues to the past, I walked around the town looking for some references to Wales, but apart from the Welsh Bridge, they seemed to be in short supply. Chester Street was there, but nothing west of Offa's Dyke appeared to have got a mention in the bits of Shrewsbury I visited, but maybe I had missed the signs. While Priory Road, Milk Street, Butcher Row and the like appeared to give a clear picture of what might have taken place in their part of town, other names were more puzzling, and as I headed for a nearby restaurant, I was still wondering what might have happened in Grope Lane.

A foppish young man had stood next to me as we waited to cross one of the town centre's busiest roads. A moment later, a grossly fat rosy-cheeked teenage girl, wearing a black shapeless top and short skirt over tight leggings, had come around a corner and waddled towards us. We had both glanced at her. For a few seconds there was a profound silence, but then, just before he sprinted through a gap in the traffic, the young man had said, 'Black is so slimming ... ' Young fops can be very cruel.

Less than an hour later, I came out of a pizza restaurant having enjoyed a tasty salad (really, they do exist), and a conversation with a retired teacher who sat at the next table and did not appear to be in a hurry to finish his meal. I had taken a well-used copy of *Scoop* from my rucksack. My fellow diner had seen the cover and told me that it was his favourite after the *Sword of Honour* trilogy. It did not take long for him to guess I was Welsh and ask why I was in Shrewsbury.

'Research, I suppose, for a book I'm trying to write.'

'A history book?'

'No, not really, more a ... '

I ground to a halt, finding, as usual, problems in defining the type of book it was – an eclectic mixture of history, language, geography, culture, politics, psychology and the like, made definition problematical. It was not a guide book or anything, but maybe it was some sort of social commentary, whatever they are. At least I had a title and when I told him about 'Offa', he seemed to like it, but perhaps he was just being kind. It was hard to guess his age, but however old he was, he was a gentleman. Unlike the man known as Barry, he had been born and brought up in Shrewsbury, before leaving for university and teaching jobs in London, the north-east and mid-Wales. His wife had died only months after his retirement, so he decided to return to his Shropshire roots. It was time to ask a question and make use of his experience. Did he think there were any real differences between English and Welsh people?

'Yes probably, when you strip away all sorts of things like personality, temperament, upbringing, age, sex and money, which part of the country they come from and all that, people should be more or less the same, but I'm not sure they are.'

'What are the differences?'

'Well they're hard to identify for a start, and they don't show up every minute of every day.'

I was listening to an intelligent, thoughtful man, who hesitated before adding more detail.

'I think they're buried somewhere deep inside us, but they probably help shape the way we look at life.'

As the lunchtime crowd thinned out around us, I asked him what he meant. He smiled in a self-deprecating kind of way, before saying, 'well it's only my own little theory, but I think it's got something to do with the migrations of the Celts.'

'Across Europe or wherever they came from?'

'Yes, before they finished up on the edge of a continent.'

'Why did they keep moving on?'

He paused before telling me that he was not an expert in the field, just had his own thoughts on the matter.

'Sometimes they were pushed, but sometimes they were drawn to places they didn't really know. Celts are wanderers, I'm not sure they like settling down – huge generalisation and all that but ...'

'But things like that can shape the way we live our lives?'

'I think so, yes – most Celts see themselves as outsiders.'

It was not difficult to think of artists, actors and musicians from Port Patrick to Port Talbot who emphasised their Celtic roots. Politicians are a different case. It does not usually take too long before MPs from the Celtic fringe start sounding like Mockneys. The Celtic cringe is alive and well, not just among politicians, but in so many other parts of modern Britain. Was Shrewsbury a 'border' town?

'Not everyone would agree, but in my opinion, yes it is – what do you think?'

For a moment or so, I thought about the question. Shrewsbury was not new to me, although writing a book makes you look at a place in a different way. It might have been something to do with a brief occupation by the Welsh some 800 years ago, or the road and rail links to places in the heartlands of Wales, but Shrewsbury, did have the *feel* of a border town. And it did have a rowing club on the Severn called Pengwern – what more evidence do you want?

'I think you're right.'

He smiled again. 'Thanks, are you going to mention Darwin?'

'Don't think so.'

'Why?'

'Three reasons.'

I ticked them off. 'Lots of good stuff has already been written about him. Wallace should have got more credit, but he was Welsh ... ' I paused and thought about their relationship.

The teacher smiled as he saw the chip on my shoulder.

'And?'

'And it isn't meant to be a guidebook.' The teacher gave a couple of slow, gentle nods before asking his final question.

'What about Wilfred Owen? Given his background I'd have thought he'd have been a good choice for you.'

Over the years I had collected my own memories of the man who was killed a week before the end of the First World War, just seven days before the bells rang out in Shrewsbury and across the land. I had thought his Welsh and English background, the fact that he was born in Oswestry, not too far from Offa's Dyke, and his family links with Shropshire, would make him an ideal subject for a page or two, but in the end decided against it. I did not know enough or write well enough to be able to do justice to the man who wrote those lines I first read in a dusty Swansea schoolroom – *Dulce et Decorum est* …

Thinking about travel, it was probably time I left to catch the bus back to Montgomery. The teacher wished me luck with the book and said he hoped I found a publisher. It was a good way to finish a stimulating conversation.

The terminus was busier than it had been when I arrived in the morning, but the woman at the information desk was pleasant and knew her stuff and I thanked her, feeling confident that this time I would catch the bus I wanted. I looked at the timetable she had given me and saw that villages along the route had names that sounded as if they had been made up by a writer scripting a Hollywood film about the English countryside – not too difficult to pronounce, but still satisfyingly rural – Crucklton, Yockleton, Stoney Stretton, Westbury, Worthen, Brockton and Chirbury. Saying them out loud made Wales seem a long, long, way away and yet at least one academic believed that a Welsh cultural influence has always affected those living to the west of towns like Shrewsbury, Leominster, Ludlow and Hereford, but still on the English side of the border. Theories like these are hard to test, and my own research and brief conversations might not be convincing, but I had my doubts. Still, as I was to find out, many complicated conflicts, involving forces which owed allegiance to leaders not countries, had indeed been played out in the lands we were travelling through on this peaceful afternoon.

The bus was pretty full, but no-one sat next to me; perhaps a warning had gone out to the travelling public to avoid contact with a writer from Gower in case you end up in print. As we began the journey to Montgomery, I listened to snatches of conversations swirling around and wondered if, beneath the superficial differences, most people, including the two teenage girls sitting behind me, wanted the same things out of life, regardless of how old they are or which side of a dotted line they were born.

In preparation for the trip, I had read about some of the villages we would be passing through, but although the results would not wow those who know their local history, it added interest to the countryside we were passing through now we had left Shrewsbury behind. Near the village of Westbury for instance, which we had reached in the next ten minutes or so, I had learned that an overgrown site marks the position of 'Caus Castle, which is part of the deserted township at the east end of the Long Mountain.' I had read the description and revelled in it. Deserted villages or towns are so wonderfully evocative, don't you think?

According to the research, one Roger le Corbet was granted several manors by William the Conqueror for his fine work during the invasion and decided to build Caus Castle on 'one of the best defensive sites along the whole of the Wales England Border'. I looked out of the window at the gently undulating countryside and was puzzled by the statement. Surely a dramatic crag or very steep hill would help the castle's defences? But what did I know; the last castle I had built was on the beach at Caswell and that did not last longer than the first few tiny waves that lapped against its sandy walls. Battles to seize the castle, named after Corbet's birthplace in Normandy – *Pays de Caux* – might serve to illustrate the complex rivalries that claimed lives and changed lives in this part of Shropshire. At one time, a *seneschal* or officer in the household of the earl of Stafford (I think!) was charged with defending the castle against rebellious forces led by Owain Glyndŵr. The officer's name was Griffith ap Ieuan ap Madoc ap Gwenwys! As it happened, after pleas from Welsh scholars at Oxford University, the *seneschal* changed sides and therefore did not have to fight against his countrymen.

I was lost in fourteenth-century battles, when the teenage girls sitting in the seat behind me, started speaking more loudly as one of them got agitated about a boy they both knew.

'He wants it soooooo much.'

'Yeah, but I couldn't ... not with him.'

Her friend sounded unconvinced. 'Because you're choosy ... right?'

'Can be.' This was a discerning girl.

'You weren't on Friday night.'

'That was different.'

'Amy said Kelz wants him.'

'Kelz can have him.'

The first girl came in with the timing of a pro, 'She already has!'

They both laughed while I smiled. It was a good way to travel.

I was still in a cheerful mood as we neared the attractive village of Chirbury. To a passing stranger, it seemed prosperous enough with its pleasant houses and shiny cars parked on driveways next to well-kept gardens. The description of the place in the *National Gazetteer* highlighted some of the changes that have taken place since the words were printed in 1868 – not just in the place or local governance, but in the way we use language today.

> Chirbury, a parish in the upper division of the hundred of Chirbury, in the county of Salop, 3 miles from Montgomery, and 18 miles SW of Shrewsbury. It is the Saxon Cyriebyrig, near Ethelfreda's Castle and Offa's Dyke. The village is very agreeably situated, in a fine and fertile valley, on the borders of Montgomeryshire. It formerly had a castle, which was said to be built by Ethelfreda, Queen of the Mercians, and its ancient consequence is evident from having given its name to a hundred.

A few minutes later we reached Montgomery – which I had always thought of as a real border town. Daniel Defoe, who had used the same phrase to describe somewhere he found 'much decayed', might not have been too impressed, but I was. Although I had been there several times before, Montgomery was still something of a blank canvas in my mind. I only knew a few facts about the town and they might have been wrong, including the belief that some of the handsome Georgian facades on Broad Street had been added to much older houses and that not far away to the east, Lymore Park was one of the very few places where Offa's Dyke, the Offa's Dyke path and the border between England and Wales coincide. But one of my abiding memories from my first visit to Montgomery was walking around a legendary ironmonger's shop – Bunners, which attracted customers and browsers from all over the country. The shop was not just worth seeing, but worth going to see.

The early showers of morning had given way to sunshine that touched the town with soft light. Distant puffs of clouds only added to my sense of well-being. If I had been wearing a stetson, it would have been set at a jaunty angle as I dawdled near the fair in the square before heading towards the little museum that lay just around the corner waiting to be explored by a man who'd had an enjoyable day. *Jaunty* and *dawdled*, two of my favourite words in one sentence, now all I needed was the legitimate use of *quirky* to complete the hat trick. Things were falling into place, because I was able to nail it in the next sentence.

The Old Bell Museum was a quirky treasure. Built in a sixteenth century inn of the same name, I moved from little room to little room enjoying the eclectic range of exhibits that tried to tell the story of the town's military, economic, cultural and social history. By the time I left I knew more about castles, Normans, railways and the way people lived in nineteenth century Montgomery. I also thought I probably knew more about the nature of the town and the kind of people who live in and around it today.

But feelings are usually more powerful than facts and a poem by W.B. Yeats, *The old men admiring themselves in the water*, which accompanied a black and white photograph of workhouse women doing their washing in the River Camlad, left the strongest impression of all ...

> I heard the old men say,
> 'Everything alters,
> And one by one we drop away.'
> They had hands like claws, and their knees
> Were twisted like old thorn–trees
> By the waters.
> 'All that's beautiful drifts away
> Like the waters'.

I thought the words were wonderful, even if when I read them, I was all too aware that soon I would be eligible for a (gulp) bus pass.

A couple of friendly and helpful volunteers manned the desk and answered my questions as other visitors wandered around looking pleased to be there. For a few minutes, we talked about the museum, the town and the type of people who live in the area. Their patience in answering my questions deserved an explanation, so I told them about my attempt to write a book about the people who live alongside the border and asked what they were like. After a few seconds thought, the man said, 'They're very ... easy going I think.'

The woman with him agreed. 'Well, they are around here anyway.'

He smiled. 'Probably because it's a nice part of the world – if most people try and be helpful it must rub off, mustn't it?'

It was, and I wondered again about the links between place and behaviour. It was too simple to say that the nicest people live in the nicest places, but I remembered the words of the homeless man in Whitchurch, 'Cities make us brutal', and thought he might have had a point.

A few minutes after thanking the volunteers, I was sitting in a small café looking at a menu. It was the kind of place where a blackboard lists the day's specials. It was the kind of place where strangers share tables. It was the kind of place where a quarter of an hour later no-one had come near to take my order. It was the kind of place to leave and look for somewhere else. All I wanted was a pot of tea.

A policeman entered the café just before I left, but the two events were not related. He was a reassuringly big policeman, a policeman from the days before they invented policing on the cheap. He was a policeman from our youth and … he was not in a car! He was walking! A policeman walking around a town.What will they think of next?

It did not take long to be served in café number two. It also did not take long to see that Montgomery must have some well-heeled inhabitants or attract visitors with deep pockets because the menu prices would not have been out of place in Knightsbridge. Three generations of the same family were sitting at the next table – grandmother, mother and daughter. The little girl was of an age to have just started school, but had yet to learn that shouting in a public place would not necessarily endear her to people who did not know her. Those who did know her however, just smiled indulgently as they enjoyed their leek and celeriac soup and the sound of the little girl's voice.

I looked, listened and thought they were probably middle-class from middle England with the attitude that said 'love me, love my child', then thought some more. Was I being too judgemental? Probably. Perhaps I should move to this easy-going part of the world, it might help me become a more tolerant human being.

On my travels, I had seen references to 'Flicks in the Sticks', but not the 'Borderlines Film Festival', which I read about as I sipped my tea to the continuing background sound of a spoilt child. Apparently the initiative, an annual event, brings films to villages in Herefordshire and Shropshire, as well as to small Welsh towns like Presteigne and Hay-on-Wye. There appeared to be more Arts Festivals per square mile in this part of the country than any other and I wondered if the presence of so many 'artists' who had escaped from London and the south-east had anything to do with it.

I cannot tell you how many times I had read publicity sheets saying things like 'Redvers grew up in Hampstead and trained as a life model under internationally respected tutor Hans Bottie, before fleeing to Little Bendover in the Marsh and founding the School of Rolfing, where he teaches High Energy Creativity and runs Green Shoots, probably the best known arts festival in the northern Marches.' But perhaps I should not rush to judgement; Redvers might be the nicest life model in the history of life modelling.

Outside, the fair was getting ready for business. Excited children were preparing to get even more excited by the brightly-painted machines that would soon be giving them thrills and memories to last until the next time. Adults stood around smiling and wishing they were young enough to join them. In this sort of atmosphere, it was not difficult to start a conversation with a man and a woman, doing their duty as grandparents, about growing up in a little border town. After a few minutes, I learned that although they had been brought up locally, on the Welsh side of the border, they had moved away after they got married and had lived in different parts of the Midlands for many years. I asked if they felt British, Welsh or none of the above. The man was the first to speak. 'British probably.' His wife agreed.

As so often in these conversations, I asked the rugby question.

'If Wales play England at rugby, would you care who wins?'

This time it was the woman who answered.

'Yes of course, we'd want Wales to win!' She looked at her husband. 'That's right isn't it?'

He smiled and agreed while I thought that nationality was turning out to be more complicated than I had thought. I had met people who were obsessed by it and others who never thought of it. Some people buried it away and only brought it out with great reluctance, while others wore it as a badge of pride. For a few moments we chatted about their grandchildren and I learned that when they were old enough, they could choose from local secondary schools or even go to one at Bishop's Castle in Shropshire. Was this true? Didn't the border mean anything in this part of the country? It was time to go to Bishop's Castle and find out.

Bishop's Castle to Newtown

IT IS HARD TO BELIEVE there could be a more pleasant bus trip in Britain, than the weekly service between Bishop's Castle and Newtown. Looking back, the omens were good. Before boarding, I had gone into a nearby mini-market and I got old-fashioned service and polite answers from a young man who sold me a bottle of water. As I paid him, I asked about local accents.

'Is it easy to tell where someone's from?'

'You mean around here, in Shropshire ?'

'Yes.'

He was nineteen and had lived in Bishop's Castle all his life. 'No, not really, I can tell if they're from Shrewsbury, but ... '

'What about somewhere like Ludlow or Leominster?'

He looked doubtful.

'Well, I couldn't but maybe someone else could.' Although I was worried about giving him the third degree so early in the morning, his good-natured smile invited another question.

'Can you tell if someone's from Wales?'

'Not if they're locals – you know, someone from just over the border ... but you can as soon as you go in a mile or so.'

In a mile or so – it sounded like going into *Stasi* territory at the height of the Cold War ...

Outside, I stood in the cool of the morning and listened to the quiet sounds of a small country town as it shook itself into life. Nearby, an estate agent advertised properties for sale on both sides of the border. Further up the hill that led to the lovely old brick town hall, a notice board displayed cards from small companies based in both England and Wales. Welsh newspapers were on sale in English Bishop's Castle. Daily life straddled the border line that separated the two countries. The day before, I had spoken to a youngish waitress and asked if Welsh people caused any problems in the town. For a moment there was silence while she thought about my question.

'Not that I know, quite a few of them live locally ... I don't think there's any trouble.'

She hesitated for a moment before giving another slant on incomers.

'But people from London and you know, the south-east can make it difficult for us.'

'In what way?'

This time there was no hesitation. 'Well they can buy houses and some of us can't – they've got money and we haven't.'

'Do they move here?'

'Some do, the others just come for holidays.'

'So they price you out ...'

A faint shadow of resignation flitted across her pretty face.

'Yes, I suppose they do, but some of them settle here and start businesses – it means jobs for people like me.'

Although I had been told that Bishop's Castle attracted not just the wealthy from big cities, but those who wanted to live some form of alternative lifestyle, on my three visits to the town, I had found that hippies seemed to be in short supply. However, assuming they were out there somewhere, weaving peace bracelets for sale to passing visitors, I could see why they might have settled here; it had the feel of a place on the edge of things, on the edge of Shropshire, on the edge of Wales and far from the bustling conurbations that lay to the east. As I waited, I glanced at a brochure which was devoted to festivals and events in Bishop's Castle, Clun and the surrounding villages, and was not surprised to find that they peppered the calendar like buckshot. Festivals appeared to be available in a broad range of colours – like the Clun Green Man or the Blues Weekend at the White Horse. There were arts events and those that required more energy, such as the Walking Festival or a Tandem Triathlon at Bishop's Castle. Perhaps I did not have enough energy, because the Clun Valley Beer Festival looked the most appealing event of all. Some had their own pleasing, but puzzling names. Why had Farmer Phil of Ratlinghope wanted to start his own festival? Wasn't Aston-on-Clun Arbor Day something to do with one of the Charles? Was it too early to think?

Luckily, before too long, I was joined by a couple of locals who were also waiting for the 773 bus to Colebatch, Clun, Newcastle-on-Clun, Duffryn, Anchor, Kerry and Newtown. They said hello, then smiled, nodded or had brief, friendly conversations with people who passed. It was miles away from the snarling world of an Eastend soap.

'Good morning.'

'What you mean good morning? Vers nuffink good abaht it … is crap.'

'Yeh … 'spose so.'

The bus driver and my fellow passengers would never be seen in Soapsville – they were too cheerful for that.

As we trundled down a smooth road that wound its way between fields and meadows that for some reason reminded me of southern Germany, I listened to the easy flow of conversation between old friends who made regular use of this weekly bus trip to Wales. Almost in the time it took me to realise that for this morning at least, I was a lucky man, we reached Clun. Just across the little stone bridge that spanned a clear river of the same name, a small group of men and women waited for our bus to stop, and as we pulled up on a road now even narrower than before, I began to understand why someone like John Osborne, who was buried in the town, would want to swap the big city for the tranquillity of a place like this.

Within minutes, I was speaking to three of the newly-boarded, and was told by one of them, a lively woman in her early sixties, that 'this bus is a lifeline.'

'What do you mean?'

'Well, to get to most other places in Shropshire, you've got to change buses, but on this you can go straight through to Newtown – we go to the market there every week.'

She half turned and smiled at her friends who were listening to the conversation, before pointing in the direction we were travelling, 'I prefer going that way anyway – west.' The others nodded in agreement – west is best, even if it meant travelling along a B road that did not look much wider than someone's driveway. The lively woman was originally from Shrewsbury,

but her family background was Welsh. Did that affect the way she thought of Wales?

'Probably.'

'Who would you support if England played Wales in rugby?'

'Wales, I think.' She sounded slightly startled.

'There's lots in Clun who wear Welsh rugby jerseys.' It was the man's turn to speak in a broad accent that I took to be rural Shropshire.

With a slow shake of the head he said, 'I canna understand that', but neither could the other woman with the kind eyes who sat next to him. She liked the Welsh and Wales, but England was her country and Clun her little bit of heaven in the hill country of Shropshire.

'Do you get many people moving to the town?'

All three took a deep breath, because some things needed saying.

'Oh yes, we get plenty,' the lively woman was the first to speak, 'too many.' The others nodded their heads in agreement.

She carried on with the fluency of someone who'd had the words in her mind for some time. 'They join things as soon as they arrive, and before you know it they start organising us.'

With a tiny smile, the second woman joined in using understated sarcasm, 'Makes us wonder how we managed before they came!'

Just after she said this, the bus came to a halt to give a small car, heading the other way, the chance to pass us at a spot where the road widened enough to allow it to do so.

'Are we far from the border?' Somehow I made it sound like Checkpoint Charlie.

This time it was the man who answered, 'No, only a mile or so now.'

'It's lovely country.'

All three beamed with the pride of locals who every week, claimed possession of the land we were travelling through.

'Does the border make any difference to your lives?'

I should have known what their answers would include the words 'free prescriptions and car parking', but I was not anticipating their regret at what they saw was the slow dismantling of the United Kingdom.

'You know, with parliaments for Scotland and Wales and all that, it's not right, is it – we're all one country, aren't we?'

Were we? I was not so sure and nor were most of the younger people I had met on my trip so far. The man spoke as we rounded a bend, 'Now we're in Wales.' I had not seen any sign, but it was a very unassuming border on a very narrow road.

The week before, I had talked to a bright, sensitive woman who had spent all her life in and around Oswestry, hopping between houses in England and Wales. She had surprised me with her view that for a fair chunk of its length, the border between the two countries was natural, and judging by a landscape that was beginning to show subtle changes, I thought she might well be right.

As the road climbed on its way to the west, the hills got bigger and shorter, paler green grass began to replace its longer, darker green cousin that had coloured the countryside we had been travelling through. I was promised that soon we would get a view to remember.

'In a few minutes we'll be on the top and you'll see what we mean.'

'It's lovely up there.'

'When it's clear you can see Snowdon.'

'Last week it was really sunny – pity it's a bit cloudy today.'

It was, but it did not take anything away from a view over the waist of Wales that took some beating. After a few minutes, we began to wind down the hill to Kerry and I asked them if they did much travelling.

The second woman was in first, 'Last weekend, we went to Liverpool.'

'Did you like it?'

'Yes, nice people, but they said we sounded Welsh.'

'I think we do a bit.'

While I listened to the three discussing their own accents, I thought back to a conversation I'd had with a woman in a Clun shop that sold drawings and paintings, mostly inspired by the surrounding countryside.

'If you look at a map, Shropshire could be a bite out of Wales, if the border went straight down, we'd be Welsh!'

Then it was back to the present as my first friend told me that 'Eight or nine will get on in Kerry.'

She was to be right, but as we neared the bottom of the incline, the chat turned to places a little further away, like Ludlow, Knighton, Montgomery and Bishop's Castle. Two of my new friends were not quite sure if Kington was English, but all three thought that the border did not really matter, because people from their part of the world all shared the same sorts of problems, regardless if the towns were in England or Wales.

After Kerry, a lovely tiny place that appeared to be content to snooze in the sun that had begun to win the battle against the grey early morning, the bus was one seat off being full. Happy people took part in multiple happy conversations as our happy little bus approached Newtown and its weekly market. At any moment, I expected an outbreak of community singing from passengers who seemed to glow with the joy of sharing the same morning bus ride to bargains, but we reached the town before anyone broke into song. Perhaps they were inhibited by the presence of a scribbling stranger. A Tuesday market had been held in Newtown since 1279. Markets which survive that long usually have something going for them and this one was no exception. It was big and busy and would probably still be in existence when the Adult Boutique (in mid Wales!) I had passed near the station, became just another faint footnote in the history of the town on the banks of the Severn.

Sometimes a stranger can see more clearly than anyone. A local sees their own personal stories written all over their town or village. The story is often a long, interlocking list of the houses, schools, shops, pubs, parks, roads, churches, gardens and neighbours they know or have known – it is a list that can blur the vision through complexity and emotion – it is *knowledge* that sometimes makes understanding more difficult. A local might not see the Newtown I was seeing. My Newtown was snapshots, theirs were movies, but haven't you ever come out of a cinema still wondering what the film was all about?

To me, Newtown seemed like somewhere on the way up. It had a range of speciality shops that suggested that the place had enough locals with enough money to buy their products. I say locals, because it did not feel like a tourist town. It did not feel particularly Welsh either, even though I heard lots of people speaking the language as I strolled past market stalls laid out along the streets. I sat in a crowded coffee shop with the name of a Welshman above the door and tried to get to grips with Newtown, Powys. For years, silly reasons had kept me away from the place. Invariably, I would skirt the town centre as I drove along the main road between south Wales and Manchester. Why? Because I hated the colour of the dark red brick that was used for some of the buildings. Any more silly reasons? Yes, once I had seen a presentation about how this part of Wales would grow thanks to public money and the efforts of thousands of people from the Midlands who would be attracted here by job opportunities and the quality of life ... think about it ... The presentation had even included artists' impressions of what Mid Wales International Airport (I kid you not) could look like in ten years time – it was something you would expect to see as you came in to land in Los Angeles.

I was still thinking back to those days when I heard a young woman with a toddler in a buggy ask if I would mind if they joined me at my table. I did not. She seemed nice and the baby seemed to be asleep. Was she from Newtown?

'No, I moved here about ten years ago.'

'Do you like it?'

'I suppose so, there's more to do here now than there used to be.'

I guessed she was Welsh speaking and asked the question.

'Yes, all my family are.' And so were many other people in the nearby Tanat Valley, where she had lived until her move to Newtown.

'It doesn't really seem like a Welsh town to me, what do you think?'

She didn't hesitate, 'Oh, I think it is, you hear the language more and more.'

The young mother looked down at her tousle-haired daughter, 'I speak Welsh to her, I think it's important.'

'Is it a *border* town?'

'What do you mean ... border?'

What did I mean? It was hard to put it into words. 'Well, does Newtown look over the border into England, you know for shopping or jobs or hospitals ...'

'I don't think it does, not in the way you mean, people go to Shrewsbury sometimes, but that's about it.'

For a few minutes, we chatted about something and nothing. As we talked in a room bright with conversation, I noticed that there were words printed on a frieze that ran around the room – Ciabatta, Rioja, Pasta, Croissants and those old favourites, Cappucino, Latte and Mocha. We said our goodbyes and I left the shop wondering what Robert Owen, the great nineteenth century social reformer, who was born in the town, would have made of it all.

On my way to a nearby art gallery, I visited what must be the most unusual and elegant W. H. Smiths in Britain. On two floors, it was a shop and museum in one. A leaflet I picked up told me it had been restored to its original state when it was opened in 1927. Outside, coloured ceramic tiles spelt out the shop's name and services offered inside – from selling newspapers to acting as a library, stamping dyes (whatever that meant) and binding books. I walked past oak-panelled walls and counters and then went up the stairs made from what looked to be the same wood, to find a small museum that told the story of a business started by Walton and Anna Smith, just three years after the French Revolution. The Smiths understood that then, as now, people wanted their news to be as fresh as possible and concentrated on the successful development of a speedy, efficient distribution chain. They succeeded, others did not. The business grew and by the middle of the nineteenth century, those living in little places like Newtown, were getting their news on the same day as those in London and the big cities. It had been an interesting diversion, but it was time to get out and about. I had a lot to discover in a couple of hours, because weekly border buses do not wait for the tardy.

In the Oriel Davies Gallery, an attractive building, just yards from the busy main street, I was delighted to find the unexpected. I had expected a couple of gloomy landscapes by minor eighteenth century artists and an exhibition of gloomy landscapes painted by pessimistic local painters, selected by their friends on the committee, but instead found some interesting contemporary Welsh, British and international art. Some of it was not for me, but I liked the white space that provided a sympathetic context, the clean, clear colours of the big prints of a Cardiff-based artist and one of the multi-media displays that showed some unusual effects of changes in light, water and sound at the bottom of an old oil drum. I was happy that the gallery probably contributed to the life of the town, but I was a grumpy old man and grumpy old men are never completely happy for long, so I left, still chuntering away inside about what I had seen written next to some of the exhibits. 'Pretentious' and something that rhymed with 'wrap' came to mind. I was still shaking my head and wondering why minor academics or art tarts use words like 'otherness' to describe some abstract concept known only to those seeking critical acclaim and public money, when a man, sitting on a nearby seat, asked me a question.

'Not happy with what you've seen?'

It was hard to tell how old he was. Was he forty going on fourteen, or thirty odd after a hard life?

'Most of it was OK.'

I was conscious that I might have been a bit more enthusiastic, so I conjured up a decisive nod as I said, 'Yes, there's some good stuff in there.' It sounded like a clearance sale at a discount shop.

It might have been hard to guess his age, but everything else was beginning to make sense – he was probably fed and watered by Arts Council money – he had that look about him.

'But you didn't seem too happy. Was it what you expected?'

I stole a quick look. I had been told not to make too much eye contact with potential nutters, but he seemed harmless enough.

'Well ...'

'Possibly a little too *contemporary* for you?'

He had quite long salt and pepper hair that was swept back and kept in place by what must have been the world's most efficient gel, because a smile stayed on his stretched skin throughout most of our conversation. His artist's clothes were various shades of black. When he spoke again, I got a rough fix on his accent and guessed he had grown up where the mountains of north-west Wales tumble down to meet the waves of the Irish sea.

'Not sure? I saw you looking preoccupied and shaking your head. Hywel notices these things.'

I looked around, but we were alone.

'Hywel?'

'Me, it's my name.'

He pronounced it the way we always had, to rhyme with Howell.

'What's yours?'

'Gareth.'

His smile grew even wider and this time it reached his eyes. He patted the bench next to him and said, 'Why don't you sit down Gareth. It's a nice day, we've got all the time in the world.'

He might have sounded like Louis Armstrong, but he was wrong, because I would be leaving town in just over an hour. Still, he might be a local. He might be able to offer some arty insights, so I sat down on the far end of the bench and got ready for sudden movements.

'I'm afraid I haven't got all the time in the world, must catch a bus later.'

My new friend became business-like, 'Right Gareth, tell Hywel what you thought of the gallery.'

'The place or the contents?'

He half turned and looked at me. His very pale blue eyes reminded me of a husky or one of those Lapp breeds you half recognise on news clips from Crufts.

'Place *and* contents.'

'I liked the gallery itself and most of the paintings or prints or whatever they were.'

'But you didn't like everything you saw?'

'No , one of the exhibits was OK – the one in an old oil drum but ...'

He held up a hand, 'Gareth, it's an installation, not an exhibit.'

'Oh sorry, but I don't suppose anyone's going to be too bothered what I call it, are they?'

'What about the artist?'

'Perhaps, but she's not here is she? And anyway, if she was, I'd tell her that I liked looking down into the bottom of her oil drum – the water and changing colours of the lights and all that.'

There was a silence for a few seconds as Hywel did some thinking. Then he sighed and said, 'Gareth, please listen, I'm going to try and remember the exact words used about the *exhibit* as you called it.'

He cleared his throat and seemed to read from a paragraph printed in his mind.

'This evocative and haunting installation explores universal and inescapable themes of loss and mortality.'

'Really? I must have missed that.'

There was another pause before he spoke again, more quietly this time, 'Gareth, are you Welsh?'

'Yes, why?'

'Are you sure?'

'Yes.'

'Because I would expect a true Welshman to have more soul. Welsh men and women are the most sensitive people in the world.'

I was starting to get a bit irritated, 'How can you say that? You get sensitive people everywhere.'

He considered my words as a small gang of sensitive, soulful, local hooded teenagers, walked past us carrying cans of strong lager, and then surprised me by conceding at least some of the argument.

'You're right, I can't say it about everyone in the world, but we're the most sensitive, creative, cultured people I know, we're innovative and ...'

He was getting a bit agitated as he tried to think of other qualities, so I made an attempt to head him off at the pass, 'Do you work in Newtown?'

'Hywel works all over Wales.'

'Doing what?'

'Performance Art, I tap into the soul of communities.'

'How do you do that?'

He smiled enigmatically, 'It depends upon the project.'

I was no wiser. 'Why don't you tell me about your last project?'

Almost before I had finished the question, he asked one of his own, 'What do you know about great paintings?'

'Well ... ' I hesitated, wondering how to answer him.

'Do you know the *Arnolfini Wedding*?'

'Yes, Jan Van Eyck.'

'Or *L'absinthe*?'

'One of the impressionists, Degas I think.'

'That's right, good ... well, I went to little villages in different parts of Wales and got people to dress up like they are in the paintings.'

It was my turn to be puzzled, 'And then what did they do?'

'They told the audience what they were thinking, they acted out their roles, they *improvised*.'

As I thought about what he was saying, he rushed on, 'Well for *L'absinthe*, everyone did some research on living in Paris at the time, then we built the set as best we could – the bar where they were sitting. Once we were ready, the actors tried to imagine they were the person in the painting ...'

'So they had to decide if it was absinthe that had got to the miserable bugger with the pipe or ...'

'Or if it was something else, and the woman might have been sad because she saw no future for herself – the actors had to *interpret*.'

His smile got even wider, 'When we were ready, we projected a slide of the painting onto a big screen, then opened the curtains and the painting came to life! It was Hywel's best project – ever!'

'Sounds very interesting, do you work in English or Welsh?'

'Both – it proved to me that I was right in what I said earlier – we're the most sensitive, creative people on earth!'

'But it might have worked in a little English village!'

He spoke with real conviction. 'No, don't think so, they're different over there.'

'Different?'

Hywel thought for a moment. 'Do you know the poem by Harri Webb?'

'Which one?'

'The one about English culture.'

He paused for a second, and then recited the words with a terrible certainty, 'Hooray for English culture, to some it's such a blessing, tuneless songs and tasteless jokes and blowsy bags undressing!'

As I watched his performance poetry, he carried on with renewed vigour, 'Philistines, the lot of them – I lived there for a year – they always got my name wrong.'

'What did they call you?'

'Hyoowel ... the bastards ... however many times I tried to tell them, they kept getting it wrong, I think they did it deliberately.'

It was time to leave him with his angst, 'Sorry, must go, got a bus to catch, good luck with your next project whatever it is.'

He nodded, 'I'm going to try and get some money to explore the concept of rejection through a refusal to engage with the world of advertising.'

Was he serious? Had I just taken part in some Performance Art? Was he just a bullshitter? I placed my own mental bet, and then waved my goodbye to the man on the bench and walked away wondering if I was right.

As the bus climbed the hill out of Newtown, I did some thinking. The place was better than I had expected it to be, but it was not somewhere I would think about with any real warmth. It was not the town's fault, but mine. Those years of irrational prejudices were too deeply ingrained for them to be wiped away after one quick visit.

Two seats ahead, I saw my friends from the outward leg. They turned around and asked me what if I'd had a good time. Newtown was great wasn't it? It seemed wrong to put a dampener on their good humour with vague, negative thoughts about the place, so I agreed that, yes, Newtown was great. They smiled and the cheerful conversation carried on until I got off the bus in one of the nicest places I had ever visited – Clun.

Some small towns just feel right and Clun was one of them. I had been there once before when early March had seemed like late May and been captivated by just about everything I saw and heard. If anything, the town looked even better today. I stood and looked at a few lively ducks playing in the clear, clean river Clun that glittered in the sunshine as it flowed through the five low arches of a wonderful stone bridge. In an adjoining little car park, the notice board and public toilet were mercifully free of graffiti and I wondered why some other places were disfigured by those who lived in them. In the spotless toilet, operatic arias were piped in and played to users in need of soothing or artistic stimulation. I strolled up the hill and found a friendly café on the quiet main street, where, over a pot of good coffee, I sat and read through a collection of local guides and newsletters and tried to get a feel for Clun.

It might have been close to the border, but I was still surprised to find so many Welsh references in such an English- looking town. A local football team played in the Mid-Wales South League and some of the nearby hamlets and farms had Welsh place names. Many pages included photographs of people called Jones, Williams, Davies, Hughes, Pugh and Lloyd. In one newsletter, I read an article about 'The Standing Stones of Clun', which contained a suggestion for the derivation of the name for town and river. The author believed that the medieval keltic (sic) name for Clun was Tre Golonwy, but through a number of steps, based on abbreviations and mutations, Clun came to be used for the town and a river of the same name. The author finished the paragraph by writing 'Nevertheless, I'm not suggesting that the council puts up a sign saying 'Croeso i Tre Golonwy, Welcome to Clun'! Perhaps he did not want that sign, but the fact that he wrote about it in the first place, underlined the border's shadowy status in this part of the world.

Getting off in Clun had seemed like a good idea at the time, but, as I left the café to see the sights, I began to think it might not have been one of my better ones, because with the next bus not due for a week and taxis likely to be an endangered species, it was a slightly worried man who began to follow 'The Clun Heritage Trail', hoping that something would turn up.

An hour later, I neared the end of my tour under a sky where most of the sunshine had been replaced by bruised clouds that were beginning to move towards us from the darkening Welsh mountains to the west. I had enjoyed my brief peek at the ancient town. Two people had borrowed a phrase and told me that it was 'the quietest place under the sun', three had seen me looking down at my trail guide and stopped to ask if I wanted directions and everyone else had smiled or said hello as I passed. This was not a place where eye contact was an invitation to a fight. I was still worried by a possible week-long wait for a bus as I walked towards the iron gates of Trinity Hospital, built in 1614, with money from the Earl of Northampton, to provide charitable accommodation for locals of 'good character'. This emphasis on personal qualities seemed to be of continuing concern for the almshouse, because in a journal, published in 1885, I had read about the duties and stipend for a barber– 'some honest man brought up in the trade', to help keep 'poor men clean from vermin', by trimming hair four times a year.

The imposing gates were gilded by spring sunshine as I ambled towards them and saw that two people were already inside – a blonde-haired woman wearing expensive, casual clothes and a tall teenage girl, who were standing side by side on a path that led to the chapel and looking at a statue of two men, dressed in what I took to be their Victorian best, which had been set in a neat and tidy kitchen garden.

The woman glanced back over her shoulder as she heard me scrunch over a patch of gravel before smiling and nodding a greeting.

'Good, isn't it?'

Before I had a chance to say anything, she turned back to the statue and spoke again. 'We don't come here very often, but each time we do, we pop in and see our friends, Billy Cantie and Joe the Bear.'

'Who?'

She pointed to the terraced cottages we could see through an archway and said, 'Former residents', before looking at her black-clad daughter with the short, boyish brown hair and giving her a gentle, affectionate smile, 'for some reason, we both like them, don't we?'

The girl stared at me without warmth, before giving a one word answer from the side of her mouth.

'Yes.'

Even my best friends would not say I was sensitive, but it didn't take much to see that the girl disliked me on sight. She was probably only about fifteen, but was nearly as tall as most men. While her mother asked me a question, the girl carried on staring at me with muddy dark eyes. It was an odd combination; attractive, groomed mothers and punky tomboy daughters do not usually go together.

'Is it your first visit to Trinity?'

'Trinity? Here?'

'Yes.'

'No.'

The observant reader might have noticed that my answers were short and to the point. It might have sounded as if I had a limited grasp of the language, but my brain was busy deciding if I had ever met these people before. I did not think so. If I had, I might not have remembered the woman, but her daughter was a different matter. Once seen, never forgotten – she had one of those sulky faces you would like to do something about.

It was time to try and ignore the girl's stare, 'Is the chapel open?'

As the first signs of an early dusk began to change the town's appearance, a glossy woman, a teenage girl and a man who was way too old to play rugby for Wales, walked down the hill towards a family-sized powder blue BMW. The woman was pleasant, the teenager angry and the man relieved because he had been offered a lift back to Bishop's Castle.

The girl wanted to sit in the front, the girl always sat in the front, didn't her mother know that?

'Yes, but you can go in the back today, Gareth is our guest'

'Look it's alright I'll ... '

'No, you get in the front, Holly'll be fine in the back.'

'Will I? I'll have to be, won't I?'

'Holly!'

The woman's voice was firm. This was a woman who meant business, but I had my doubts if she would keep it up. She gave me a brief apologetic smile, 'Sorry, she's usually very nice.'

I smiled back and said, 'I'm sure she is ... ', but thought that Holly was probably only nice if she got her own way.

As we drove back across the bridge and turned left for Bishop's Castle, I learned that the woman had been brought up in a peaceful Berkshire village, but now lived somewhere in the Vale of Belvoir. She had gone to a private school as a day pupil, but Holly had recently started boarding after getting a bit of stick from the girls at a local comprehensive ... even though it was meant to be a good one. The mother was nice, classy and trusting – she must have been trusting to offer a stranger a lift within an hour of meeting him for the first time. They had come up for a few days to stay with her mother who had moved to a bungalow somewhere past Bishop's Castle, just over the border in Wales.

'But we're not Welsh,' she said, a bit too hastily for my liking. 'Not that I've got anything against the Welsh, of course.'

The voice came from the back seat. 'I have, I don't like them.'

'Holly!'

'Sorry mum, but I don't – I wish Grandma didn't live there.'

It was time to ask a question, I had a book to write. 'Why don't you like Welsh people?'

The girl hesitated, and then gave me her reasons, almost as if she was ticking them off a list

'They're not the same as us, they sound funny and they're usually small and a bit furtive ... '

I looked across at the Sulk's mother who was about to say something and said, 'It's OK; I'm interested in finding out why Holly doesn't like us', before half turning to glance behind, 'what do you mean by furtive?'

'They sort of wheedle things out of people.'

'What sort of things?'

'Money for a start, they want things both ways.'

'What do you ... '

The girl broke in before I had finished asking the question, because her list was far from exhausted.

'They want us to pay for their medicines and that silly little parliament thing in Cardiff – we pay for everything , we pay for their Welsh language ... '

It was my turn to interrupt, 'Who's we?'

'People like my parents and our friends.'

I pulled down the sun visor and adjusted the mirror so that I could see the teenager with a bad case of Youthful Certainties. 'Oh, what was that about the Welsh language?'

'I read something in the paper the other day – it said that we pay millions of pounds to keep the language going just for a few shepherds in the hills.'

'It might be a bit more complicated than that.'

'I don't think it is. The Scots are the same, we give them everything but they don't like us.'

'Some probably don't but ... '

The woman glanced towards me and said in a proud maternal way, 'Holly's always been interested in politics and current affairs, haven't you, darling?'

As the Brute in the Back agreed, we neared Bishop's Castle and I saw the dreadful outbreak of road signs that disfigured the approach to a charming town.

'Where shall I drop you off?'

'Anywhere, thanks.' The sooner the better – you have been nice, but your daughter could get a bit wearing.

The car stopped, but I wanted to ask her a question before I got out.

'Do you agree with Holly?'

'Well, not all of it ... '

She hesitated, did some thinking, and then spoke again.

'I know some very nice Welsh people. We had them round for supper once.'

Remind you of anything? As the big car moved off into the distance, I wondered if I was being a bit too sensitive, but it had been a very long day.

Kington to Knighton

THROUGHOUT MY JOURNEY, I was to find out that information about rural buses was usually given out on a 'need to know' basis. While all around me people were going about their lawful business, I spent hours following instructions from a *Dalek* and pressing the one, two or hash key until I felt like lying down and listening to Leonard Cohen. Human beings were the most helpful, but it was often difficult to find one, so when I had a chance to speak to the driver who was going to take us between Kington and Knighton, I was confident I would get the information I wanted. After all, if he did not know the details of the return trip, who would? I told him my research suggested that one afternoon service terminated in Presteigne. To get between Presteigne and Knighton, I would need to book something called a 'rural taxi', but the nice man in the council's travel office did not seem too sure about the details. Could the driver help? There was a pause.

'Well, afternoon timetables are ... *difficult.*'

'Difficult to understand?'

There was another pause while he thought about what to tell me.

'I don't know, they're just *difficult.*'

This was time to choose my words with care. 'Can I get a bus back here from Knighton?'

I could not recognise his accent, but it did not seem to be local. He spoke slowly and thoughtfully, 'Only if you get the early one. I'm not too sure about the taxi ... I think you've got to book it the day before.'

'Is it subsidised in some way or have you got to pay the proper taxi fare?'

He seemed troubled as he said, 'I'm not sure.'

Nor was I, but I got on anyway and was still thinking about the timetable for my return journey from Kington to Knighton, when the Happy Hippy got on the bus in the middle of nowhere. She paid the driver, then looked around and smiled at us all. It was a beatific smile of certainty that made even a grumpy old man like me feel better about living in a Britain where contestants on television reality shows are the inspiration behind a range of perfumes or they open dog shows. It might only be a few weeks to Easter, but I could see she was no spring chicken as she took her time deciding where to sit. Her lined, reddened face probably got its colour from hours in the open air planting vegetables for her family and I knew that little Moonbeam and Sioux had grown up as healthy children, thanks to the vitamins in the organic crops she teased from the land that surrounded a little cottage filled with brown rice and love.

Who would have thought I could have worked out all that from a quick glance at a woman wearing a mustard fleece, rainbow socks and dark glasses, carrying a woven bag sporting a sticker that told the world she was against nuclear power? As she sat down a few rows in front of me, I could see long grey hair that hung in uncombed natural swirls from beneath a multi-coloured knitted woollen hat and wondered if I should go down the bus to talk to her. It might not be a bad idea; at least it would get me further away from the middle-aged whistler who was sitting with his wife on the back seat. Both wore matching grey-green anoraks with thin navy-blue stripes. Both spoke in accents which could have earned them a few bob as extras in a long-running soap opera that was set somewhere east of Sloane Square. Say no more. They had been there when I boarded in early morning Kington, which was, unusually, an English town on the western side of Offa's Dyke. I had sat in front of them, only half aware of their murmured conversation, while we waited for the scheduled departure time. Then, as if machine and man were linked, the bus had started at the same moment a breathy whistle emerged through the man's moist lips. After a few bars, I recognised the *Marseillaise*. To begin with, it had been a mildly pleasant surprise. The anthem had not taken long and before we had left the red bricks of Kington, he had moved seamlessly into *Drink to me only with thine eyes*, while I thought it made a nice change from listening to one-sided mobile phone conversations conducted by people who say things like 'Yeh, right, we'll get pissed togevvah.' You do not hear much whistling these days, but within a mile, the novelty had begun to wear off. It was very odd, because every time the bus stopped, so did he. I did not know if he was programmed in some way, but I was reasonably sure his wife was probably deaf and that he probably worked alone, far away from colleagues who might wish to do him harm.

The bus had moved smoothly through lush countryside, while he moved through his repertoire which included a repetition of the first eight notes of Beethoven's Fifth. See if you can stay calm while you run them through your mind a few times ... da da da dum ... da da da dum, pause, da da da dum, pause, da da da dum ... I could not , but I still believe that one day, I will get an NVQ in Tolerance. You have to hold on to a dream. But such pinpricks did not matter on this bracing morning and although I might not be as happy as the hippy who was now swaying dreamily into corners as if she was a passenger on a pillion, I was still a contented man as I watched the bus underline its importance to the lives of some of those who live in this part of rural Herefordshire.

Before the journey, I had thought that everyone who got on would be going to Knighton, but I was to be wrong. A sweet-faced little old lady who might have come from Central Casting, got on the bus clutching a large envelope, then got off in Titley, as did a young mother with a calm and docile little boy. The same old lady boarded on the way back, this time without an envelope. I assumed she had been to the village post office (if it still existed), before visiting a friend who baked wonderful cakes and brewed her own wine. It was that kind of place. I was sure that far away from this fresh, invigorating day of scudding clouds and easy-going winds in the Welsh borderlands, in plush offices found deep within the post office's London headquarters, fat cat senior staff were even now working on a strategy to tell carless young mothers and little old ladies in rural communities like this, why closing their local branch is really a *very* good thing for everyone concerned.

As our bus headed for Wales, we passed an ugly stretch of flailed hedgerow. I do not know if hedges, maintained by human hands rather than machines, are now too expensive to even consider, but I did know that if some of the rural roads of Britain are not to be submerged under drifts of pulverised twigs, the skills needed for success in Young Farmers' Hedging and Ditching competitions, should be valued, not just by the judges, but by us all.

I must have blinked and missed the sign welcoming me (and presumably everyone else) to Wales, but on the outskirts of Presteigne, I saw bilingual signage and knew we were in a different country. Later, I spent some time in the town, and was attracted by its placid charm, but for now at least, the driver had a timetable to follow, so after a pause at a stop outside a recycling site to pick up three new passengers, a man and two women, we resumed our journey to Knighton.

The man, who was probably in his late seventies, was wearing a Chicago Bulls peaked cap. Had he still been alive, my own father would have been only a few years older. Had he still been alive, my father might have wondered why I was roaming up and down the England/Wales border trying, unsuccessfully, to talk to compulsive whistlers and pensioners from Radnorshire who wore caps with the name and logo of American basketball teams ...

I could imagine the conversation when the Bulls fan got to Knighton and spoke to his caring daughter.

'You alright Dad?'

'Yes, I am now, but there was a strange man on the bus who ... '

'Who what?'

'Who was, you know, weird.'

I could almost see his daughter's troubled face, 'Weird? What do you mean weird?'

I could almost hear her father's soft country burr, 'He wanted to talk about basketball or something.'

'Basketball?'

'Yes, that was it – basketball and borders.'

'Borders as in flowers?'

'Don't know, I pretended to be deaf and he shut up.'

Within a couple of miles, it was obvious we had left the soft leafy lands of rural Herefordshire behind. The road climbed above valleys which were steeper than they had been on the other side of the border. My map told me that we were approaching Offa's Dyke, but my eyes saw no sign of it as we approached the top of a hill and prepared for our descent into Knighton – *Tref-y-Clawdd*, the town on the Dyke. I had chosen to take a bus between Kington and Knighton, to find out if there were real differences between two towns in two countries separated by only a few miles and a couple of mischievous letters. I had already drawn some conclusions about Kington, but proper comparisons and contrasts would have to wait until I returned from today's trip and spent some time in both.

As we reached the outskirts of Knighton, I began to recall faint memories of driving through the town when I was young, sharp and could still touch my toes. After those depressing thoughts, I looked more closely at the jumble of buildings ahead, and began to appreciate the problems of trying to get to grips with the differences between perception and reality. Before my visit, the place had got mixed up in my mind with other border towns like Ludlow, Bishop's Castle and Hay-on-Wye, towns where locals and tourists might feel at least a flutter of anticipation as they wandered around looking in the windows of interesting shops and restaurants, but as I walked through Knighton, I started to think that this was somewhere which had probably seen better days and hoped I was wrong. With only the sound of my footsteps for company, I strolled up and down streets that might have once have buzzed with light and life, but now seemed strangely muted. Empty shops cried out for new money and those shops that were open, cried out for new customers. I hoped that someone would tell me that I was seeing the town on a bad day – 'Come back tomorrow, the place will be jumping', but somehow thought that I was going to be disappointed.

As a quick rain shower made the pavements slippery, I made my way to the library and was glad to find that it was quiet. There was no contradiction involved. Although towns should be lively, libraries should be filled with hushed voices and the wonderful smell of books, not the sound of loud conversations, the ring tones of mobile phones or the noise of people eating a packet of cheese and onion crisps. But people who thought like me were losing the argument in towns and cities all over Britain, as many libraries became Happening Information Centres and those in charge spend their time ticking political boxes. For a few moments, while I stood in the vestibule and looked at notices promoting events, polite users passed me to choose or return books in the room beyond the half-open door. Although an eclectic range of interests was on offer, from an 'Introduction to Mothing' (was 'Mothing' a word that had slipped in under the back door?) to a call from artisans for empty, coloured wine bottles to turn into stained-glass windows, I still did not get the impression of a town bursting with energy.

A polite, helpful woman answered a question I had about a venue, and then told me, not without a certain sadness, that a lot of Knighton's 'oomph' had

drained away in recent years.

'It's a pity really, because there are a lot of very nice people who live around here.'

I asked her if she was a local. 'Yes, I was born just the other side of the border, but my family's Welsh.'

'Are you Welsh?'

The woman thought for a moment. 'I suppose so, but it's not that easy, things get a bit mixed up around here.'

'There's no animosity then?'

'Don't think so.'

I did not say anything and waited for her to continue.

'No, don't think there's any trouble, the town's had a lot of knocks, but I've never heard of problems because people are Welsh or English.'

I think I understood what she meant – economic hardship sometimes triggers a search for scapegoats.

Within minutes, the pleasant, knowledgeable woman brought up the two hot topics of the day – free prescriptions and free hospital car parking in Wales. I was not surprised; those awkward twins had dogged my progress for the last few months. My informant told me that local people were sometimes sent to hospitals in towns like Shrewsbury, but recently, Welsh Health Authorities had been slow to pay their bills. The conversation drifted on to the Assembly Government in Cardiff before I asked a last question – the one which asked which way the town faced.

'Can't speak for everybody but ... ' The woman paused and then told me what she thought. 'I think we face east into England to places like Ludlow and Hereford, not west into Wales. If there was a big Welsh town near here, it would probably be different.'

As we finished our conversation, she said she hoped that whichever way Knighton faced, it would start looking to the future.

'Hay's done it, the clock in Hay's the same as the one here.' She pointed down the road to the town square and the tall clock, now temporarily covered by scaffolding.

'If they can do it, so can we.'

I hoped she was right, but set off for the Offa's Dyke Centre without any conviction that she was. Perhaps my expectations were too high. I expected to find the centre jam-packed full of information, but instead, found a circular room with some illuminated panels, a few photos, a couple of bilingual touch screen animations that looked as if they were aimed at children, a gift section, and a number of books about walking the length of the dyke. I doubted if most visitors would spend much time in the place unless it was raining. But perhaps my expectations were unrealistic and my criticisms unfair. After all, what did I expect to find – Offa's Dyke scholars studying samples, a section of the dyke itself, rooms full of satellite photos and copies of research papers? Whatever the reasons, I still left the centre with a sense of disappointment and suspected most visitors would have felt the same.

Luckily, within minutes, disappointment had been replaced by the stimulation of good conversation. In a nearby shop, I met a good-humoured and interesting man who told me that he slept with his head on the Welsh side of the dyke and his feet on the other. With a fleeting image in my mind of someone who lived in a tent straddling a grassy mound, I asked where his heart lay.

He smiled as he said, 'In Wales, the line of the dyke runs through the town and through my house.'

I gestured towards the counter and a pile of literary magazines, written in English by local writers, and asked if I could buy a copy.

'Of course, have you seen it before?'

'I looked through it earlier.'

'What did you think?' For some reason, he seemed a little anxious.

It was easy to tell the truth. 'Some of the poems have got a real feel for the language.'

'One of mine's in there.'

'What's it called?'

When he told me, I remembered the piece and was not surprised; his Welsh roots showed through his grey hair.

'I enjoyed it'. It was not pretentious, but there was a lot of deep stuff going on beneath the poem's few, simple verses.

In half an hour, we covered a lot of ground. He had lived in Knighton for a long time, but had been born in industrial south Wales. We both agreed that Welsh people loved not just words, but the *sound* of words, before moving on to the reason for my visit.

'Knighton's a real border town.'

I thought I knew what he meant; in this case, 'border' was probably not just a political and geographical reality, but an attitude of mind.

After thinking for a few seconds he said, 'I don't think there's any serious trouble between the Welsh and English,' and then smiled, 'although if you walk down through the town when Wales are playing rugby, the roof almost comes off the pub when we score!'

Another customer came into the shop and started browsing. My guide to Knighton looked across at him, and then spoke again.

'When I arrived here, it was a real agricultural market town with a population of about eighteen hundred, and lots of labourers worked on farms on both sides of the border, but things have changed.' He said it with a hint of sadness.

'In what way?'

'The population's grown for a start. I think it's over three thousand now, mostly people who came here to work in engineering factories built in the sixties.'

I suspected I might have known the answer before I asked the question. 'Where did they come from?'

'Mostly from the Midlands, but you know what it's like, places close or they lose staff and it has a knock-on effect for everyone'.

'Any other changes?'

'The usual in somewhere like this, more young people leave to get jobs than come to live here.'

Not that I was young, but I had to leave soon, so I asked if he thought there were any real differences between Welsh and English people, or was it just a cosmetic camouflage of leeks and tired music hall jokes. As I had come to expect from a bright, sensitive man who had done his share of travelling, he weighed up the question before answering, then gave me two anecdotes that to him illustrated at least one difference.

Not that long ago, he went to the funeral of a man who was either a farmer or farm worker (it was difficult to clarify the point when he was in full flow), in a small village not far from Knighton. The church was packed and many mourners found themselves outside listening to the service on loudspeakers. Everyone joined in singing the hymns and no-one worried about any possible embarrassment, even though the ones outside were not somewhere where they were meant to sing or *safe* to sing, like the inside of a church. They just sang in the open-air surrounded by both strangers and people they knew.

'Do you know what I mean?'

'Yes, I think so'.

I have been to funerals with forty in the pews but only three or four singing. I had seen mourners mouth silent hymns while others stared down at the words with the fake concentration of a sphinx. If you caught their eye, they usually gave a brief, forced smile and then pretended to gear themselves for the next verse which never came.

'Have you read *On the Black Hill*? It was filmed around here.'

I knew the book, but not the film or play.

After telling me he had met Bruce Chatwin in Knighton, he said that he was in the audience when *The Black Hill* was on in Builth and people joined in when the actors sang. It was 'very Welsh.'

'But they sing in England.'

'Yes, but do they enjoy it as much?'

It was his turn to ask me a question.

'Why are you interested in all this?'

I told him about the book.

'What's it called?'

Without speaking, I found a scrap of paper on the shop's counter and wrote down the title. He looked over my shoulder and laughed.

'Now all you've got to do is write it!'

Finishing the book seemed a distant prospect at that moment. 'Yes.'

He paused for a moment while he thought about what I had said. 'How can you find out about somewhere if you only spend a few hours there?'

Other people had asked me that. 'I don't suppose you can, but sometimes the longer you spend in a place, the less you know it.'

'And everyone who lives somewhere will probably have their own view of the place.'

It was my turn to agree, 'Yes and anyway, as I keep telling people, I'm not trying to write a travel book or anything.'

'Good luck with it, and if you need any more help ... ' He left the sentence incomplete, but I knew what he meant.

I was just turning to leave when he asked me a question.

'Forgot to ask – you been to the Space Guard Centre?'

'No, should I?'

'I would, it's not something you expect to find in a place like this.'

He was probably right, but I had a bus to catch. There was always tomorrow. As it turned out, tomorrow never usually comes, but some time later, it did.

As we left Knighton, pale sunshine flickered over the hills we were about to cross, while I thought that nowhere looks quite the same on a return journey. Maybe I was becoming more alert, because this time I did see a wooden signpost for the Offa's Dyke path and wondered if I would ever walk its length. I thought about it as we began to drop down towards Presteigne and came to the conclusion that it was probably a bit like heavy gardening or becoming fluent in French – thinking about it was more attractive than doing it.

The rest of the journey passed with only the sound of the engine providing the background noise as the few remaining passengers stayed silent in their seats. I was beginning to feel hungry as we approached the town and hoped that Kington's food matched the sheer excesses of its promotional material.

As those who have read this book from the beginning will know, ever since I can remember, I have enjoyed looking at brochures and leaflets promoting the charms of towns, villages and areas interested in attracting tourists, through the symbiotic twins of pictures and words. Over the years, I have revelled in the sheer *chutzpah* of claims that bear little resemblance to the reality. You know the sort of things – enticing photographs of golden sands that turn out to be a sliver of dirty grey beach or shots taken from varied angles of the only interesting building in town. But in my opinion, nothing can compete with a brochure written by someone in love with prose that flows into the madder upper reaches of fantasy.

With this background, I was thrilled to come across a glossy flimsy which told the world about 'Kington – one of the great small towns of Britain', which I read while sitting on a bench near the bus station. What a find! It would have an honoured place in my collection of purple sudsers, but as you might think differently, I have picked out a couple of phrases and sentences, so that you can judge for yourself.

'Kington is an elegant specimen of a post-Medieval market town, still in everyday use (what does that mean?) by some of the descendants of the people who built it. It manages to avoid being pretty by being beautiful.'

See what I mean?

Or what about 'Kington is small enough to be in touch with itself, but big enough to be excellent ...'

My own favourite acknowledged local circumstances, 'In many small towns, the twenty-first century means a rash of familiar high street shop fronts. Not in individualistic Kington – a shopper needing to eat, drink, build, farm, celebrate, dress or buy furniture need never go in to a chain store – unless the chain began in Kington.'

As I walked along an unremarkable town centre road, looking above a collection of roofs to some green hills and farms which 'produce some of the finest sheep and cattle in the Kingdom', I did not know that within minutes, I would meet a man who would hold me personally responsible for spending his hard-earned income. I was buying a few bananas and chatting to the woman behind the counter, when the two way conversation became three. The well-built, middle-aged man opened up the attack with a question.

'Why should we subsidise you?'

For a few seconds I wondered what was going on. I looked around. 'Me?'

'Yes, you're Welsh, aren't you?'

'Aye, from Gower.'

He nodded as if he knew. 'It's your accent; thought you were, I heard you saying you'd been to Knighton.'

'Just come back, went by bus.'

The newcomer's next few words sounded like the start of a limerick. 'A talented young baker I know ... '

From his tone, he was either one of Kington's less contented citizens or more generously, was having a bad day. There was a brief pause as he struggled to hold back strong emotions before starting again. 'A talented young baker I know wants to open a bakery but ... ' While I waited for more, he seemed to be calling on reserves of anger which would be used to propel his words through the air between us. 'If he sets up in Knighton, the Welsh government will give him a grant, but if he sets up in Kington he'll get nothing!'

'Yes but ... '

'It's true!'

'Kington's not in Wales, so how can ... '

'But my taxes go to the government and then the money's sent on to Wales, so I'm working to pay Welsh people to open businesses!'

While I was weighing up the pros and cons of going down the old macro-economic route, he was off again.

'Why should my money help someone start a business in Knighton when he would prefer to start one in Kington, it can't be right!' I began to recognise that most of his sentences ended with exclamation marks and thought it was time to fight back.

'But no-one gets any say in how our taxes are spent.'

'But we should!'

'Yes, probably, but it's a bit more complicated than that.'

I looked at him and wondered if I should leave it there, then decided I could not.

'Look, the Government wastes my money on all sorts of things, that's what governments do!' My own exclamation mark might not have been as forceful as his, but at least it was a start.

He moved a step closer. 'What sort of things?'

'The London Olympics, counselling classes for illegal immigrants and terrorists, diversity officers, the bin police, plastic surgery for paedophiles, MPs' expenses, the BBC – you name it they waste it.'

I could see I had struck a chord. His expression told me he was not too happy that his money was going to be poured into that financial black hole known as the London Olympic Games, but his next few words told me that he was even more upset that any of his money was going to be spent in Wales.

He pointed to the west, 'Over there, they have grants for *everything*!'

'I don't agree.'

'Everything's free in Wales – free prescriptions, free car parking, free bus passes ... '

I tried irony in an attempt to stop his flow, 'A land of milk and honey ... '

'Yes! Paid for by me!'

While I had an image of the people of Wales lying around on soft cushions, being fed peeled grapes and drinking fine wines, he brought me back to reality.

'I went to Merthyr once, what a place, all those tips – awful.'

'With not a pint of milk or spoonful of honey to be seen!'

He hesitated, and then smiled the smile of someone about to win an argument, 'Ah, but that was *years* ago, things have changed, they've got rid of the tips and now they're opening businesses, on my money!'

I couldn't win, so changed the subject, 'Do you go to Knighton very often?'

'Not if I can help it!'

As an undercover reporter for a mass circulation Sunday newspaper might have said, 'I paid for my bananas and left', hoping to find a restaurant or a pub with an interesting menu.

It must have been my lucky day, because I did not have to make any difficult decisions. The town might well have a 'green heart of park and playing field', and be somewhere 'cars are usually left unlocked', but I was not spoilt for choice when it came to finding somewhere nice to eat.

In the end, hunger pangs drove me into a place where the plastic flowers on the tables had not been changed since 1963, about the same year the baked potato was put into the oven. I would guess the potato had been removed after a few months, then kept in a freezer for decades, until it was taken out and put into a microwave next to what the menu outrageously claimed was bacon, before joining what was impishly described as salad on my plate. I had a few mouthfuls, looked around at walls painted the colour of a tart's lipstick, before giving in to an irresistible urge to get up, go outside into the fresh air, eat a banana and some biscuits I kept in my rucksack. A couple of minutes later, I was sitting on my old friend, the bench, reading a local paper, jotting down a few notes, sketching the buildings opposite and wondering if I had been a bit hard on the town. Alright, my meal had been truly awful and the man who knew a talented young baker might have expressed his opinion in a more sensitive way, but there seemed to be plenty to like about the place. I was reading a few articles that suggested Kington held its fair share of concerts, shows and festivals when someone spoke to me.

'Do you know how long it will take us to get to Brecon?'

The dark-haired woman, wearing an oatmeal coloured top and calf-length skirt, who asked the question looked like she had just come off a fashion shoot for very expensive, casual clothes. The tall man with her looked like he could pay for them with his loose change. In the last of the afternoon sun, I squinted up at the pair and tried to call up a mental map of this part of the country.

'I'm not from round here so I'm not *really* sure – are you driving?'

'Yes, the car's over there somewhere.' She waved an elegant hand in the general direction of everywhere. Deep blue eyes, light tan, nice voice. Perhaps she did all the talking, maybe he was the strong, silent and very rich type with a good taste in women.

'Which way would you go?'

I thought some more. 'Well there's a road that goes from Hereford towards Brecon past places like Whitney and Hay-on-Wye … think it's the 438 … that might be best'

'How do we get to the 438?'

'Head towards Eardisley, can't miss it, it's the way I came in – Brecon should be signed somewhere along the line.'

'Seems quite straightforward.'

She added some explanation. 'My satellite thingy's not working.' I was just beginning to tell them that at this time of year most garages were selling cheap road atlases, when the man broke his vow of silence.

'How long will it take?' From the way he asked the question, I thought this was a man who would always want accurate answers.

'Not sure; don't think it's that far, just under an hour perhaps.'

The rich man looked at his pretty woman. 'Should be OK then … drink? For the moment, she ignored his question, if that was what it was. From what I had seen and heard so far, it could have been an order.

'What are you drawing?'

'Not much, just a few impressions of the place.'

I stood up and began getting my things together.

'Why?' There are no fabulous prizes for guessing who asked the question.

She looked interested, he looked irritated and I tried to look like a sensitive writer.

'It's something I do to remind me of somewhere.'

'Why don't you take photographs?'

'Haven't got a camera.'

The tall man seemed puzzled. 'Then why don't you buy one?' It was the right moment to shake my head and give him the fleeting shy smile of a sensitive writer who had a lot on his mind.

'Haven't got time, too much planning to do.'

'Planning for what?' He seemed surprised that people like me ever needed to plan anything.

'A bus trip.'

It sounded like I was going to Cape Town via Paris, Madrid, Marrakesh, Cairo, Kinshasa and Nairobi.

The woman stared at my little rucksack, which had just enough room for a small water bottle, a note book and some crushed biscuits. 'A bus trip where?'

I tried to look like an intrepid traveller. 'From Presteigne to Leominster.'

My rich, tall friend repeated the sentence as if he had misheard what I had said. As they both still seemed to be perplexed by the whole business, I told them about my ambitious journey.

'I'm writing a book and need to do some research.'

'But what's the book about?'

Constant practice was beginning to pay off and in a remarkably short time I had told them why I was trying to write 'Offa'.

'Sounds interesting.' I smiled; there's *nothing* quite like encouragement from a very attractive woman.

'Thanks, right, I'd better go ... hope you find Brecon.'

With a little smile on her flawless face, she said, 'I hope we find our car!'

Then, after a sideways glance at her man, the woman asked me if I would like to join them for a quick drink. For some reason, he did not look as if he had spent his whole life waiting for this moment to arrive. As both stared at me, I wondered if I should, but then, inexplicably, agreed, and within a very short time, the three of us were sitting in a lovely old coaching inn chatting away as if we had known each other for at least ten minutes. I cannot pretend that it was a relaxed, easy conversation, because it started on a low note and then went downhill.

I had only just had my first sip of orange juice, when Patrick (for that was his name) began to complain about the problems of buying 'somewhere in the country'. Apparently, in the past few months, they had been doing some research, as well as spending the odd day here and there, actually looking at potential houses, but so far had not bought the place of their dreams. I decided to play a full and constructive part in the conversation.

'Where do you live now?'

'North London.'

Somehow I doubted if it was on the top floor of an old stained tower-block where the lifts did not work and packs of teenagers and dangerous dogs run wild.

'Do you want to move out of London, or will it be a second home?'

Patrick looked at me with an expression of distaste. 'I don't like the term second home, it sounds greedy. Other people might use it, but we don't.'

The woman with no name looked uncomfortable and hastened to counter any whiff of snobbery that might be hanging around our table.

'We don't think we're better than anyone else, it's just that we've got used to saying we're looking for somewhere in the country ... that's all.'

'Any particular parts in mind?'

'Not really, just somewhere we can relax when we get the chance.'

She leant back, smiled at me, and then used both hands to brush the hair back from the sides of her face. 'As long as it's got what we want, it could be anywhere, that's why we're here, having a look around, and it's on the way to Brecon.'

Patrick didn't want to be left out of things and made an effort to be polite. 'We want more information before we start arranging visits and all that.'

'Are you making much progress?'

He shook his head. 'No, we've found a few houses that might be suitable, but there's always a problem.' His mouth tightened before he said, 'Can't do this, can't do that, and don't get me going on National Parks.'

'Can't do what?'

'Build extensions, knock down a few barns that are falling to pieces anyway – you know, planning problems, political problems, silly little problems thought up by silly little people.' I am sure that for those who knew him, Patrick had a soft, tender side, but for those who did not, he came across like a hanging judge.

'Is Kington a target?'

'It might be, but we don't want somewhere *in* a town, but somewhere *near* a town, a country town ... '

There was still an enigmatic smile on his woman's face 'So places like Kington, Ludlow, Leominster might have what we want as long as they *feel* right – Patrick's a bit different, but I don't always need hard facts.'

'What about Brecon?'

He gave a short, sharp laugh. 'No chance.'

'What's wrong with Brecon?'

As Patrick prepared to tell me, his pretty woman came in with some soothing words.

'There's nothing wrong with Brecon – Tim and Suzie have been quite happy there.' She spoke confidingly, 'We're staying the night with them.'

He spoke loudly. 'They want to move out, said it was too quiet!'

'But they live there full-time, that makes it different.'

If she meant what I thought she meant, I could sense their views might start getting me a little bit on the irritated side. In an effort to maintain harmony, I decided to clarify matters.

'Do you mean there's not much to do in Brecon?'

Deep-blue eyes hesitated, 'Well ... '

'Why did they go there in the first place?' I suspect there was a bit of an edge to my voice.

While Patrick stared, his woman gave me an explanation. 'Tim's mother left him the house and they run their business from there these days, but they are thinking of moving away.'

Her man gave a snort which somehow managed to tell me – see, I told you so! I began to doubt if Patrick and I would ever become firm friends: it was time to change the place, if not the subject, back to the present.

What did they think of Kington? This time, Patrick was the first to speak.

'Not bad I suppose, but I'm not sure it's quite us, needs more shops, speciality shops, and a few really good restaurants.'

I thought for a moment. 'But you can get those in London. Don't you want a place in the country because it *isn't* in London?'

Patrick stared at me with real dislike in his eyes. 'I don't think we need you to tell us what we should be looking for in a house.'

Why had she invited me for a drink? Why had I accepted? I knew I should not keep asking myself questions, but it was hard to stop thinking about them.

'Sorry, didn't mean to cause any offence.'

Before Patrick could say anything, his woman smiled and told me I had not.

'That's right, isn't it darling?'

Patrick's assurance that he had not been offended would not have fooled a slow five-year-old. I knew it was time to offer to buy them another drink. I knew the offer would be refused. I knew it was time to wish them well in their quest for a place in the country. I knew it was time to go. As I walked away from the brief encounter, I was still wondering why the woman had suggested I join them for a drink. It had all been very odd. Anyone reading this far might have their own opinion. If they have, please let me know.

But it would be unfair to leave the reader with a false impression of Kington. It was not somewhere I fell in love with at first sight, but I did meet and talk to nice people who made some perceptive comments about the differences between their town and Knighton. From what I was told, there was no question of the place having some sort of dual identity – Kington was 100% English and that was that.

Earlier, I had read a tourist brochure promoting north Herefordshire's 'Black and White Village Trail'. According to one Alec Clifton-Jones (who is he?) it was 'unrivalled in England' and although I had not followed all the forty-mile circular trail that included Kington, his comment seemed to have at least some degree of credibility. The brochure's final paragraph, which told readers that the area was 'quintessential rural England', reinforced the feeling I had that Wales was a long, long way away, rather than just up the road.

I left Kington with the feeling that unless it was part of their job, or someone fancied a day out on the Welsh coast, most people rarely strayed across the border. Wales was another country beyond the blue mountains to the west, somewhere slightly secretive and anarchic, somewhere they did not quite understand. It was not personal; they hoped I understood.

Presteigne to Leominster

L ESS THAN THREE MILES from the dyke itself, the mellow stone walls and buildings of the county town of Radnorshire were lit up by a sun which had made the welcome decision to come out and help make my day. Within minutes of arriving, I thought that staff, writing for a national magazine, who recently chose Presteigne as one of the best places to live in the UK, might have had a point. In winds light for a weatherman to call a zephyr, sunshine made sharp shadows on clean streets dotted by polite, happy people strolling past attractive shops and pubs which looked as if they had lived a little. It was better than an episode of the Waltons.

I asked for directions to the town's landmarks, and was given answers in an accent that reminded me of the West Country, before settling down with a coffee and speaking to a newly-retired teacher who was interested in local history.

'Accent was one of the first things that attracted us.'

His came from somewhere deep within the sprawl of south-eastern England. Just after getting married, he and his new young wife decided to go on a walking holiday to the Welsh Marches – a word I did not hear too often on my journey south to the Severn and, as they say in tourist leaflets, fell in love with the place.

'Can't remember why we decided to base ourselves in this area – luck, picked it out with a pin.'

He was a tall man, with quite long greying hair brushed straight back from a bony face that was still lightly toasted after a recent trip to Morocco. With his brown-checked casual shirt and rimless glasses, he gave the impression of being an academic with a love of the great outdoors. It only took a few minutes' conversation to realise that this was a man who was interested in *everything*. There was so much to learn, and so little time in which to learn it! I was on to my second coffee before I began to get to grips with the speed and delivery of his sentences. When he was particularly excited, he missed out words that took up too much time.

'We shouldn't be in Wales drinking these', using both forefingers in succession like a child shooting pretend guns, he pointed to our cups, before carrying on at high speed, 'because we're on the eastern side of the dyke, the Mercian side, English side ... strange ... should be in England.'

'But we're not.'

'History's tied up with England.'

I think he meant the town's history was tied up with that of England, but it was a second or so before I found my guess had been right.

'Things happened in England changed Wales.'

Get the idea? It's simple, just fill in the blanks – things (that) happened in England changed (things) in Wales. They still did.

'Border's there ... ', he swivelled in his chair and shot one pretend gun in the direction of Kington, before turning back and carrying on with increased urgency to tell me more about the place he had known for the past thirty-five years, 'but round here no barriers, no mountains, no big river, travel easy, people wandered, people mixed, people had the same problems – Wales, England – same problems no difference, still no difference ... '

When he eventually paused for breath, I managed to get in a question, 'So the border doesn't matter?'

He grimaced. 'Shouldn't but it does.'

'Why?'

'Big issues affect everyone – food, water, shelter, peace, pollution, borders shouldn't matter anymore but they do.'

I could see him gearing up for a tour of universal hippiedom and knew it was time to try and tie him down with a few specific questions.

'Are there any differences between the people who live over *there* ... ', as I spoke I pointed over my shoulder in the general direction of the hills of mid Wales, 'compared with the ones who live over ... *there*'. It was time to show my versatility – the second 'there' was accompanied by raised eyebrows and a nod towards the east.

His conclusion did not take very long to arrive. 'Probably are.'

'What do you mean?'

He seemed reluctant to speak. It was as if he did not really want to listen to what he was about to say.

'Well, further into Wales people are a bit different, to do with the language, want to protect it.'

'But around here?'

While my guide to Presteigne did some more thinking, a stocky teenage boy, wearing a red fleece with the three feathers of Wales, sat down at the next table and glanced through the menu with the look of someone who had missed his breakfast. I wondered what he would make of the man who finally told me, 'A lot of people here are Welsh, some English, some neither.'

What did he mean ... neither?

'Where they're born doesn't matter to them.'

'Border people?'

'Labels don't help us understand, labels bad for us.'

Then, because he was a nice man who did not want to end the conversation on a downer, he rushed me through a brief review of local history. He talked about Llewellyn besieging a town that now found itself in Wales, Owain Glyndŵr's famous pillaging tour of the Welsh Marches and of a curfew bell, first heard when Shakespeare was a toddler, that is apparently still rung today. After a pause for breath, he told me about the town's Welsh name – Llanandras, so called because of the place was originally dedicated to St Andrew and the way the Black Death had touched the town and ended many lives.

Then, against the background buzz of other conversations, my guide gave me some examples of local dialect he claimed was still used by some elderly people – unty tump (mole hill), glat (a hole in a hedge), how bist thee? (how are you?), before bringing me up to date with features of recent arts festivals and the wonderfully named annual cycling event – the 'Tour de Presteigne'.

I thanked him, bade him farewell and returned to the peace and quiet of the world outside. To me at least, the town seemed prosperous enough, but appearances can always deceive the casual visitor who is all too ready to be taken in by appearances. I had been told that Presteigne was full of refugees tired of the daily battle to survive city life, but as I strolled along pavements and peered through shop windows, the voices I overheard could have come from the Archers.

At the end of one street, I looked to the east and decided that while any self respecting geriatric jogger could have reached the English border during a television advert break, the town felt Welsh. It was more than bilingual signage, it was something else, something less factual, but I didn't know quite what.

A few hours later, I indulged in one of my favourite pastimes – an early evening pint in a quiet pub. A man and a woman, obviously in the middle of a slightly one-sided conversation, walked into the room just as I was thinking about Philip Marlow sitting in a Californian bar at the same time of day, when the ash trays were still clean and the ice cubes had yet to melt. But Presteigne was not Pasadena and the woman who asked me a question while her husband got the drinks, was not Lola Montez. If pushed, I would have said she was a Susan, but you can never tell these days.

The voice came from the next table. 'Getting hungry?'

'Yes, starving.'

I was not actually *starving*, but some tantalising cooking smells were beginning to waft in my direction.

'Food's good here.'

'Is it? Might have something later.'

The woman smiled and spoke to her husband as he walked over to their table carrying his pint and a glass of multi-coloured liquid topped off by a mini beach umbrella and assorted vegetation that he placed in front of his wife.

'I was just saying the food's good here.'

The man gave the matter some thought for a moment before giving a one word comment.

'Usually.'

'What do you mean *usually* – you never seem to leave much!'

She turned back to me and spoke again in a voice loud enough to make me hope she never shouted while I was in the neighbourhood.

'Don't listen to him, he eats everything – never leaves a mouthful.'

Her husband gave me a wry smile before sinking half his pint as his wife asked another question.

'You alone?'

'Ah, yes.'

She pushed a spare chair back and invited me over. Twenty minutes later, I was glad she had. Forty minutes later I was beginning to have my doubts. In that time, I found out that they lived locally, he rationed his words like coupons, but she had strong views on most things that affected their lives, including the fact that they had been unable to start a family. As the bar got a little busier, the woman had tried to tell me why they failed.

'He couldn't, you know, there weren't enough ... '

I broke in before she got too deep into the problem. It was one of those occasions when it was better not to know.

'Must have been a difficult time.'

'It was, they did tests and everything – in Hereford.'

She turned to her husband for confirmation. 'They did, didn't they?'

'Yes.'

I looked across the table at his big, square face, decided he got through married life by giving few clues about his feelings and was glad not to be married to a woman who was on the verge of giving a complete stranger graphic details about their sex life. It was time to change the subject.

'Do you mind if I ask you a question?'

Both shook their heads, but he was the one who answered. 'No.'

Maybe it was his turn to speak.

'You're both Welsh right?'

'Yes, both born in Wales to Welsh parents, why?'

'Do you really *feel* Welsh living here?'

'So close to England?'

'Yes.'

He understood what I was after. She might have been wondering why her husband was so talkative, but this time was the first to reply.

'Well we're Welsh like but ... '

In the bubble of silence that surrounded our table, I waited while she seemed to choose her words with more care than usual.

'But not as Welsh as some people, because we don't really speak the language.'

'So you think that makes you less Welsh – that's what you mean?'

'I suppose so.'

I had heard the argument before and I was to hear it a few more times on my cross-border ramblings. Some twenty years ago, a language activist had told a couple of us who could only say the odd *shw mae butti*, that we were not *really* Welsh – it was a pity blah blah, and of course it was nothing against us but ... We had discussed the issues over a few beers and ended up agreeing to disagree after I asked him if the most fluent Welsh speaker, with the biggest Welsh vocabulary ever known, was the Welshest person in the history of

Welshness, but all he said was, 'It depends where you live.' What did he mean? After muttering something about linguistic purity, he shuffled off leaving us to feel as if we had let our country down, but anyway, back to a pub in Presteigne and another question.

'Do you *feel* Welsh or British?'

The woman hesitated then said, 'British probably, because we speak English', as she looked towards her husband expecting confirmation. For a fraction of a second, the man hesitated, as if thinking about consequences, then turned to me and said with a touch of defiance, 'Well I feel Welsh.'

I looked at his wife and saw her mouth set as she prepared to argue the toss; it was time for another drink and a change to less potentially divisive topics of conversation.

The next day, in the tranquillity of a mid-Wales morning, perhaps a dozen people waited for the bus to Leominster. From their chatter, it seemed as if a few were regular travelling companions, but it was hard to be sure in small country towns where manners are not yet on the endangered list. A few yards away, a tall, thin, round-shouldered man stared down at the mobile phone he held in one hand. Something about the minute movement of facial muscles and the seriousness of his expression told me I was looking at an addict. If I was right, the man's waking hours would be dominated by his phone. He would probably fret in hilly places like this where reception could be a problem and avoid, if at all possible, going to events where requests are made to turn off mobiles. Vicars can be so selfish. It is usually easy to spot an addict. They come out of supermarkets pushing a trolley with one hand and texting furiously with the other as they walk blindly across the road to the car park, 'Jules says luv … after Corrie … Gavin's out tonite (sorry about using the apostrophe – it's just habit) … U home later?'

I was still thinking about a study which looked at how addicts coped when their mobile phones were taken away (not very well apparently), when the bus arrived for the forty-five minute trip to Leominster. As usual, I was slightly taken aback by our speed and as usual, everyone else appeared to think it was normal. Rural buses are *fast*, or at least seem to be seriously fast to occasional passengers like me. Maybe fat passengers are banned from the Presteigne route, because there was plenty of room for everyone and everything, including my rucksack which was able to sit next to me, rather than my occasional travelling companions, Mr Fleshy or Mrs Huge. Across the aisle from me, the addict stared down at his mobile phone, oblivious to the attractive countryside we were going through, while I wondered if he was fretting about not being able to use it. Why couldn't he use it? Although he might well be an addict, he was probably a very polite addict, unlike some of those we see and hear in public places these days.

A few weeks earlier, along with everyone else on a bus heading for Shrewsbury, I had listened as a young man sitting somewhere behind me, with a voice that made a whine sound good, used a mobile phone to speak to Samantha and asked her to search for something. He started off with variations of 'please Samantha ... please Sam ... just look for it ... please ... come on Sam ... it must be there ... I'll phone you back ... just look for it ... please ... ', while at least one passenger wondered what Samantha was looking for in her flat and why my travelling companion seemed to be so worried. I see some of you have already got your own thoughts on the matter ... By the time we had reached the hospital on the outskirts of town, the unseen young man had been getting desperate. His voice was worried, his words were worried and I knew he was thinking of trying a different approach. Just before Darwin's house at Frankwell, he had chucked in a couple of swear words and the hint of a threat. When that seemed to fail, he threw himself on her mercy and was saying things like 'Sam, I'm late for the job centre ... I feel terrible ... pleeeeeease' as we pulled into the bus station and I stepped down onto a Shrewsbury pavement with a feeling of relief and hoping that Samantha would spend the rest of the morning choosing lottery numbers.

But luckily, our journey to Leominster was not to be spoiled by a ... (fill in according to mood or upbringing) using a mobile phone, and we drove along the green-hedged roads to the sound of murmured conversations and little peals of laughter. It was all so pleasant and what is wrong with that?

Villages are meant to be small, but maybe they breed them big in Herefordshire, because Shobdon was a fair old size. I had looked at its website before my trip and learned that Shobdon was 'renascent', as efforts to bring more life and facilities into the village appeared to be working. A well-written newsletter told readers that only a year or so ago, the local primary school was threatened with closure, the pub was on its last legs, the playgroup was struggling and the WI as dead as the parrot in the Monty Python sketch. But things had apparently changed for the better and the fortunes of those organisations listed above had improved. The flight to the cities might bring benefits to some of the individuals concerned, but overall, the thought of countryside filled with deserted villages, and drivers more used to concrete than cows, sniffing out brown sign 'attractions', made me want to buy a retirement home in a little pirate compound on the coast of Somalia. Shobdon's newsletter might have been well-written, but it still carried an article by Sir Roy Strong which included the following sentence, 'The bishopric of Hereford is a hideously over-churched diocese.'

There was so much wrong with this – from a whiff of metropolitan superiority, to the choice of 'hideously' applied to something as harmless as the number of churches in a diocese. According to most dictionaries, 'hideous' means horrible, frightful, shocking, ghastly, grim and the like. Hideous injuries, yes; the number of churches in a diocese, no. And what can I say about the dreadful 'over-churched'? Nothing that can be repeated in the pages of a book that might be read by children. Luckily, the newsletter finished on a more uplifting note with a piece about Shobdon's Home Guard during the Second World War and a reference to a local aerodrome. The word took me back to a time when libraries were quiet, women actually *looked* through sunglasses and train stations had yet to be imported from America. Anyway, these days the aerodrome is used for leisure flying and social events, but apparently, in the early part of the Second World War, pilots from No 88 Squadron RAF, flew Douglas Bostons from this now peaceful part of Herefordshire, or so I am told by Comrade G. J. Morgan.

The website also runs a bulletin board, which on the day I looked at it, featured a request for dog walkers and the news that someone wanted to sell three male rats and their cage. I hope some dog walkers came forward and the rats found a good home, preferably without cats.

In the few minutes it took to reach Eardisland, I realised that ever since leaving the border behind on the outskirts of Presteigne, Wales had vanished without trace. In other parts of England that found themselves near Wales, I had seen houses called Trem-y-Mor or Bryn Celyn and signs pointing to villages with names that reflected a Celtic past, but in this part of Herefordshire, it seemed that past was a blank page.

A number of people were waiting at the bus stop and a quick mental calculation suggested that there was a chance that one of them would sit next to me. I was right, but it was not Mrs Huge who sat down, but a stick-thin elderly lady with kind grey eyes. She was friendly and seemed happy to chat away as if we were old acquaintances. I gathered that she had lived in and around this bit of Herefordshire for most of her life and could not imagine living anywhere else. What did she like about it?

'Oh, just the usual things I suppose – the people, the villages, the countryside, you know.'

And for some reason I did. Take Eardisland. It was more than attractive houses and a wonderful bridge over the clear, clean River Arrow. It was more than tall trees that, on the day I passed through, swayed in the gentle wind like slim, sexy women, more than interesting well-kept gardens, more than inviting pubs and shops where even a stranger might get a welcome; there was something else – a sense of place. This appeared to be a contented village, but I might have been wrong. Maybe underneath, passions seethed. You can never really tell, can you? After a few minutes, and with a trace of embarrassment, the little old lady asked me a question.

'Are you Welsh?'

'Yes, from Gower.'

She looked a little puzzled.

'It's in south Wales, to the west of Swansea.'

She still looked puzzled. 'Is it a village?'

For the next mile or so, I spoke about Gower's charms with my usual enthusiasm for the most attractive place on earth (in my humble opinion anyway), while my new friend nodded encouragingly.

'Is that where you live?'

'No.'

'Why?'

'Circumstances.'

Nothing was said while we both thought about my words. Across the aisle, the addict stared at his phone; across the road a man and a woman smiled as they chatted near a car parked near the entrance to a field. It was time to ask a question.

'When I say 'Wales', what comes to mind?'

'What do you mean?'

We had reached Pembridge, another lovely village, just as I finished telling her about my attempt to write a book based on what I saw and heard as I caught buses between towns on either side of the Wales/England border. The explanation appeared to have given her more confidence and she now spoke with some assurance.

'Holidays – holidays in Wales, that's what I think of.'

'Because you used to go there for holidays?'

She didn't hesitate 'No, I've never been to Wales.'

'Never?'

A shake of the head. 'No.'

Her answer took me by surprise and there was surprise in my voice as I tried to get the reasons for her choice.

'Then why did you … ?'

I hesitated and she finished the question for me.

'Choose holidays?'

'Yes.'

There was a little smile on her face as she said, 'Probably because I saw an advert on television the other night, and there have been things in the paper about weekend breaks in Wales.'

I hesitated while I thought about what she had said. Surely a woman who lived so close to Wales would have an opinion about it – some recollection of things she had seen and heard? But apparently she did not, and her answer taught me a lesson; not everyone has an opinion about everything. It was time to ask other questions.

What did my friend think about tourists visiting her part of the world?

'I don't mind, we've got some lovely villages around here.'

'Like Eardisland?'

She hesitated for a moment, as if what she was about to say might be thought boastful.

'Eardisland, my village, Pembridge – lots of them.'

As the driver eased out of a corner, I glanced across to see a smile flicker over her face, while a couple of houses hid the morning sun, but left no trace. By the way, the rhyme is an accident, and does not represent any intention to curry favour with the *literati*.

While the addict (remember him?) stared down at his phone, everyone else smiled away like old friends as we reached the neat and tidy suburbs of Leominster and headed towards the centre of this town of some 11,000 people. I said goodbye to my new friend with the kind grey eyes and hoped I would meet more like her on my journey towards the Severn.

Leominster was not touristy pretty, was not perched on a high hill with spectacular views of the surrounding countryside, was not particularly famous for anything that I knew about anyway, did not sit astride a major river or nestle next to a lovely lake, but I liked it on sight. It *felt* right and it was a happy man who got off the bus at its terminus next to a supermarket, with a spring in his step and a plan in his head. I would buy a local paper and then read it in the first café that looked promising.

Training facilitators did not exist when I was young, but nor did other jobs like cleaning operatives or celebrity WAGs. Things change. Jargon changes. We change. We get older. We get more cynical. Anyway, on the day I read it, the *Hereford Times* carried job adverts for a training facilitator and a learning support manager. As I glanced at job details, I recalled a conversation with a teacher who wanted her school to be renamed a 'learning incubator.' Why?

'Because our job isn't to *teach*, it's to support learning, to help the growth process, to *facilitate*.'

There it was again, facilitate, right up there with comfort breaks and breakout sessions.

But why incubator? Her tight face told its own story, 'I've told you, incubators provide the right conditions for our students to *grow*.'

Make up your own minds; I had not grown enough to judge. I only went to a school.

Other things had changed since my far-off Swansea childhood. I had always thought of Herefordshire as being a traditional rural county, but I might have been wrong. As I sipped a welcome coffee, I flicked through the rest of the paper and found a 'twenty-page special', listing the names of entrants for a 'baby of the year' competition. Of course, Mercedes, Riley, Ferrari, Harley, Destiny-Hope, Summer, Bailee-Jo, Jadon-Jon, Delicia, Crystal, Blu, Lacie-Lou, Angel and the like might well be traditional Herefordshire family names that had been handed down through the centuries, but for some reason, I had my doubts. There were also a few babies with names that suggested a Welsh background – Elwyn, Ellis, Lewis, Rhys and Sian, as well as surnames like Griffiths, Williams, Jones, Powell, Morgan and Edwards that could have been taken from a Llanelli telephone directory.

An article headed 'Officers want to trace man' caught my eye. Apparently, police were looking for the person who stole a 'brown Afro-style wig', valued at £99, from a Hereford shop. Two clear CCTV pictures accompanied the article. Yes, you read that correctly, two *clear* CCTV pictures! For those who might want more detail, one showed the young man from the front, while the other had caught him turning sideways. In the first, he held what was either the wig or a less likely explanation, a bushy, black furry creature. I wondered why he had stolen the wig, but could only think that for some reason, he wanted to look like a young Michael Jackson. We all have hobbies.

Towards the back of the paper, I came across a section which listed the latest news from local villages, some with wonderful names like Ocle Pychard, Much Cowarne, Stretton Sugwas and Mansel Lacy and wondered about their derivation. Who would not? Most of the listings were in Herefordshire, but others came from Gloucestershire, with a few, such as Presteigne, Knighton and Hay-on-Wye, even straying across the border into Wales. This broad regional approach continued in the sports section, which included details of cricket matches played between teams from both sides of the border such as Talgarth and Herefordians, who both competed in the GB Liners Marches League. The paper might have had adverts for chatlines and website design, but there could be no doubt it served a predominantly farming area. By the time I had finished reading it, I could have entered *Mastermind* and answered questions on fat stock prices and tractors through the ages. Just as I was studying 'Don't make a pig's ear out of farming terms', a glossary of names and descriptions, a man sitting facing me at a nearby table asked me a question.

'Found something good?'

I looked up to see a dark-haired man in his early thirties who was wearing a thick brown coat which seemed much too hot to keep on inside.

'I saw you smiling, so I thought you must have found something good, people usually smile when they see something good.'

He kept nodding as I pointed to the glossary and gave him an answer.

'It's just a list of farming terms.'

'But they made you smile – you did smile, didn't you?'

'I must have.'

Something told me to keep things short and sweet.

'What were they … what have you seen … what were they?'

A flicker of excitement passed over his pale face while I wondered if I was talking to someone with the odd problem or two.

'I don't know, oh alright, words like weaners.'

He looked interested. 'Weaners? What are weaners?'

'Apparently, they're young pigs weaned from their mother.'

My explanation seemed to trouble him. He paused for a few seconds and then asked another question.

'Why did you smile? You smiled when you saw weaners.'

'I like the sound of the word.'

It was time to leave. My pale-faced pal might well be very nice, but something told me it was time to leave. Repetition must be catching.

I stood up, put my pad and newspaper in my rucksack and said, 'Must go, things to do.'

His question stopped me as I walked to the door.

'What? What are you going to do?'

'Try to learn a bit more about the place.'

'Which place?'

'Leominster – 'bye.'

'Do you have to go? Do you have to?'

'Afraid so.'

I left behind a man who looked as if I had kicked him in a sensitive part of the body and walked down the stairs feeling like a complete bastard.

So far everyone had been very friendly, including the woman who, a few minutes later served me in a small shop on yet another Broad Street and responded to my questions about local accents. I asked her if she could tell if someone came from Leominster.

She hesitated, and then answered. 'Probably.'

'What about Hereford?'

'Not really.'

I wondered about Shrewsbury. It was in the next county, but far enough away for accents to be different – at least they would be in Wales.

The woman frowned while she thought about it. 'Don't *think* so.'

A regular customer came into the shop, but the woman must still have been thinking about her answer after the customer had taken his change and gone.

This time she was more decisive. 'No, I couldn't, but some people could.'

'Do you know if someone's Welsh?'

'Usually, although we don't get that many in here.'

I thought she meant the shop. For years I had driven through Leominster, but the road skirts the town and generally I had only stopped for petrol. Other Welsh men and women must have done the same.

It began raining as I walked towards a Tourist Information Centre in Corn

Square. The rain was not heavy, but it did not make dawdling an attractive option. As usual, I found a helpful member of staff. She was not from Leominster, but had family roots in the town. She might not have been from the town, but seemed to like it well enough.

'I love it here.'

'Why?'

It did not take her long to think of a couple of good reasons. 'Everyone's friendly and there's a lot going on I suppose.'

My question about the recession's effect on the area produced a positive response.

'Well, some people and businesses have suffered, but it's not all doom and gloom, we've got our success stories!' After a quick diversion to Ludlow and the way it is viewed in Leominster, I asked about local words and phrases. Were there any?

It did not take her long to come up with 'Ow are you bab?' and 'Ers bin late.' As she wrote them down for me, I wondered if they would still be used in the decades to come. Local phrases have a habit of disappearing with the death of grandparents old enough to remember Bruce Forsyth in black and white. We chatted for a few minutes about the book I was trying to write, before I collected some brochures outlining the attractions in this part of north Herefordshire and then left to stroll around the streets of Leominster.

Under the finest of gentle rain that began to fall again after its little rest, I walked around trying to get a feel for the place. It was not easy. I saw a number of references to the Midlands, but to me it felt like the small Herefordshire market town it was. Perhaps it was too far from the border, but apart from a Welsh flag fluttering from the roof of a car, I could not find any traces of Wales. Leominster seemed as English as it is possible to be. I went in and out of galleries, high street and specialist shops, including ones that sold antiques, looking and listening for clues to the type of town I was visiting, but did not end up much the wiser. By the time I got back to the Tourist Information Centre to ask more questions, a man had joined the helpful woman I had met a few hours earlier. They both told me that Leominster was a 'border town'.

'Really?'

My tone suggested doubt. The middle-aged man must have noticed it and hastened to expand the statement.

'Well it's in the Marches anyway.'

His colleague added more. 'That's one of the ways we promote the place, as somewhere in the Marches, near Wales.'

For a minute or two, we talked about some forthcoming events, but I was beginning to feel hungry and thirsty, so after thanking them, I went to look for a pub. I had finished my bar snack and was enjoying my pint when two young women asked if anyone was sitting at the next table. I moved some of my gear, apologised, and they sat down. By the way, how old is a young woman? It turned out they were second year students at a university in Leeds. Both were local(ish), friendly, opinionated (a good thing when you have a book to write) and, as the final blessing, one of them had even been born in Wales. As they did not seem to be in the middle of an intense conversation, I took my chance and asked if they would mind answering a few questions. It must have been 'Be nice to Strange Men Day', because they agreed. For a start, neither of them thought of Leominster as a border town, nor as somewhere in the Midlands.

'Well, do you think of it ... in the Marches then?' Accompanied by some synchronised head shaking, both said 'no'.

While I thought of my next question, the one born in Wales, a natural blonde (they do exist) said, 'Those kind of things aren't really relevant today, not to young people anyway.'

What did she mean?

'We lead different sorts of lives.'

Her friend broke in. 'We're not so bothered about where we live as long as we're happy.'

She added helpfully, 'Young people want to be happy.'

But didn't everyone?

It was the blonde's turn. 'I'm not sure, most old people just seem to grumble about their lives. They don't even *try* to be happy.'

Her friend did not want me to think that all oldies were miserable buggers, because she said, 'Some of them try, my Gran tries, she likes a laugh.'

'So does mine – *and* she still lives in Wales.'

It was a slightly nettled Gower boy who asked 'Why wouldn't be she happy just because she lives in Wales?'

'When I go back, I meet a lot of unhappy people, but my Nan's lovely – she smiles all the time!'

I had a vision of a smiling bent old woman walking down a dark village street, where the only things that moved were twitching curtains and sheep with sad eyes. On a hill above a boarded-up chapel, a handful of people dressed in sombre clothes watched her progress as they stood under weeping skies and wondered why the happy woman still lived in Wales.

'Do you feel Welsh?'

The blonde thought about it for a second and then said, 'No, I suppose I've lived here too long.'

For a few minutes, we talked about the concept of being British. They both believed that the countries on these islands are drifting apart and that before too long there would be an independent Scotland, followed not long after, by an independent Wales. In time, Northern Ireland and the Republic would become one country. It was as inevitable as the relentless march of technology. I asked what made them angry and got a long list which included child and animal cruelty, lazy lecturers and the problems of understanding crazily complex pricing structures when trying to buy cheap train tickets. As I too had struggled with the madness of the latter (remember Rail Voyager tickets can only be bought, providing you have proof of identity, which includes a Rail Voyager Membership Card, between twenty-seven and sixty-three days before your journey, as long as it is a leap year and you want to travel on 29 February), I empathised. We talked about the way technology influenced their lives, but when we moved on to twittering or tweeting, I thought it was time to go. You can have too much information.

Just up the road I saw a shop which seemed to be worth a visit – Border Books. The owner was a nice, intelligent man who had only lived in Leominster for a couple of years. He had moved from London for a number of reasons, not least because the daily battle to travel around the city had worn him down. Was he glad he had made the change?

'Yes, my friends thought I was mad at my time of life (he looked about the same age as me – gulp), but I'm so glad I did.'

'Don't you miss anything about London?'

He thought for a moment. 'No, not really, it was great when I first went there in the late sixties, but I was young then and London was a very different place.'

I flicked through some of his stock, while he told me Leominster felt like home, he had already made lots of friends and nothing would drag him back to the big, bad city. As I listened, I glanced at a book of very good photographs of the countryside in the Marches. Inside the just jacket, I found something

that provoked feelings somewhere along the line between irritation and anger. I read that the area covered lay on both sides of the border, and that the scenery was some of 'the finest in England'. See the problem? In case some people might be wondering why I was agitated, I had better explain. Given the author had told us the Marches straddled the border and included countryside in both countries, why did a sentence finish by claiming that the 'scenery is some of the finest in England.' Forget sophistries, England had been used for both England and Wales. Was it a trivial point? Probably. Was it worth getting agitated about? Probably not, and yet …

The shop's owner must have read my face because he asked if there was a problem. I tried to tell him, but when I had finished, I am not sure he had really understood.

'Some people say England when they mean Britain, or the UK, or England and Wales, or England, Wales, Scotland, Northern Ireland and the Republic as well!'

He hesitated and then said, without any real conviction, 'Yes, I see what you mean.'

But did he? Maybe you have to be a sensitive Celt or an over-sensitive Celt to understand. As I did not want to put a nice man in an awkward position, it was time to change the subject. Did he miss London's cultural riches?

There was no hesitation. 'Not really, if there's something on I want to see I just get a train and stay with friends.'

I told him that when I had lived down there, I always planned to go to things, but usually never quite got round to going. He smiled. He knew. He had missed things himself. Sometimes the effort was all too much. Did Leominster offer much in the way of festivals and special events? With more than a trace of local pride he said, 'Oh yes, plenty, we've got a good festival, art shows, concerts ... ' He smiled. 'I'd say enough for most people.'

I asked him if he had been to Presteigne, or any other nearby town in Wales, but he had not – running the book shop took up most of his time and energy. For a few more minutes we chatted away about Leominster, before a couple of potential customers appeared in the doorway. It was my cue to leave. I smiled my thanks and left to spend more time in a pleasant interesting town, not far from a border which kept such a low profile that it might have been dug by miners.

Hereford to Abergavenny

ON A WARM, HUMID SUMMER'S EVENING, I sat at a window table in a pub that was getting busier by the minute and watched a skinny, thirty-something man, sporting dark hair streaked with crude blond highlights, struggling to get his open-topped VW into a tiny space between a brute of a black 4 x 4 and a dirty white van parked on the road outside. The man, who was going forward a touch, then back a touch, watched *Top Gear* wearing a Ferrari baseball cap and thought that actually holding the steering wheel is for wimps who did not know the difference between a late model XR 327 S and an XR 327 Si. As he would say, 'Real men, real macho men, use the flat of their hands ... *capisce?*'

How did I know all this about someone I had never seen before? Believe me, with men like him, it's easy. Along with half the population of Hereford, I listened to the pounding music he had chosen to add to the effect, and decided his name was Peter Poser. Then a sudden movement attracted my attention. It looked like parking was going to be the least of Peter's problems, because a bald-headed bruiser was hurrying towards the scene as if he was on a mission, a violent mission. A few yards behind him, his tiny blonde Barbie girlfriend tottered along on heels high enough to make it likely she would require some help dismounting from them. The bruiser did not look like the van driver, but he did look like the man who owned the shiny new 4 x 4 that was in imminent danger of being damaged.

'This could be interesting.'

The voice came from my left. I turned around and saw a tall, well set-up young man watching the unfolding scene outside with a gentle, amused smile and an air of expectation. He wore a sage-green shirt, fawn cavalry twill trousers and gave the impression that the event had been put on for his personal entertainment. Almost as soon as I turned back to watch, things started to happen. The VW nudged the car behind, the bald man shouted and the poser belatedly realised that it was time to leave while face and the posemobile were still intact. And so, just before the bruiser arrived shouting an interesting mixture of threats and promises, the VW roared off leaving behind a mixture of smoke and fear.

'Pity, I'd have bet on the baldy – what do you reckon?'

It was the young man again. 'Same as you, but the odds wouldn't have been any good.'

He laughed, told me he was waiting for Claire, who was always late, and asked if he could sit down. There was room and he might be a local. 'Of course.'

For a couple of minutes, we chatted about Baldy, Barbie and the Poser before moving on to the minds of those people who put signs all over their cars telling passengers not to bang the boot down or even think of eating and drinking when they travelled with someone who understood the importance of maintaining a clean and tidy vehicle. Sage-green was confident, articulate and a good listener. As we talked about men who always cleaned their cars after a shower of rain, I began to suspect he was a normal human being which, if true, would make a welcome change from some of the eccentrics I had met so far. Eventually, he asked what I was doing in Hereford.

'Finding out a bit more about the place.'

'Why?'

In the growing hubbub of noise I said, 'Trying to write a book.'

'On Hereford?'

'Well, yes, and other towns as well.'

He appeared interested, so I told him about 'Offa' and my plans to visit Abergavenny the next day.

'I might be able to help, I grew up here. What do you want to know?'

'What's Hereford like?'

There was a moment's hesitation while he thought about my question. 'Well some people think it's a bit of a backwater, but others think that's a good thing – depends on what you want out of a town, I suppose.'

'Is it a town or a city?'

He thought for a moment and then said, 'Bit of both, funny status really. Most of us call it a town.'

'Are they a friendly lot around here?'

'The usual I suppose – some are, some aren't.'

'How long does it take to be accepted?'

Sage smiled wisely. 'Oh, after twenty years, neighbours might say hello.' He paused and then said, 'No, I'm exaggerating, maybe fifteen.' After a few seconds' thought he told me they were a pretty stubborn lot in these parts.

'They take their time over things, but once they make up their mind it takes some changing – if they like you they'll do anything to help you.'

'And if they don't?'

Sage laughed. 'Then God help you!'

'Do you think of Hereford as a border town?'

For a moment Sage gave the matter due consideration, before giving his opinion. He nodded as he said, 'Yes, I think I probably do.'

It was my turn to do some thinking. 'Do many Welsh people live around here?'

'Not sure about the numbers, but there's a lot of Dai Morgans in the phone book – sorry, didn't mean any offence.'

He was a polite young man. It was my turn to smile. 'None taken.'

Hereford always gives problems to people like me who like to place places. Officially, it appears to be in the Midlands, but I have doubts about that little bureaucratic pigeonhole. My own word association for Hereford would include cider, apples, rural, bulls, red earth, racecourse and farms. Leaving counties like Warwickshire and Worcestershire aside, to me the Midlands means machinery, cities, houses, roads and ... you get the point.

I asked Sage what words he would choose. 'Are you talking about the town or the county? You said Hereford.'

What did I mean? 'Both probably'

'For Hereford itself – family, friends, work, home, sport, pubs, clubs, shops, restaurants, girls, neighbours, cathedral, river, racecourse, parking. Then for Herefordshire ... ', he paused for a moment before saying, 'villages, farms, fruit, apples, cider, bulls, hills – oh, and more pubs.'

I asked him to tell me more about Hereford's relationship with Wales.

'It goes back a long way, don't know much about that bit – I think it was used by one of the Henrys as a base against Owain Glyndŵr or some other rascal.'

A sideways smile told me he enjoyed his choice of words.

'What about the relationship today?'

'Well, there's a Hereford Welsh social club. Well there was – still might be going and someone said that one of the colleges here runs Welsh-language courses.'

He sipped more beer before bringing the past and future together. 'I know that a few people think the western part of Herefordshire should be in Wales, because it used to be or something.'

Sage saw me looking puzzled. 'I read it on a local message board a few weeks ago – BBC I think, not sure though. You could always look it up.'

I could and did. More of that later, but now it was time to thank him and leave; his attractive dark-haired girlfriend had arrived, smiling apologies. After brief introductions, I finished the last of my beer and then pushed through the mass of generally young men and women, high on hormones and ready for the chase, to the less crowded world outside. An hour later, I found that Sage had been right; there was indeed a message board with lots of unexpected responses to the question, 'Herefordshire in Wales?'

Apparently the debate had been triggered by a man who farms on the Herefordshire/Wales border who claimed the county would benefit if it became Welsh. He appeared to base his argument, not just on grants which might then become available, but by other, less tangible support which might follow. The piece ended, 'we always look over the border to Wales as they have a Welsh Assembly that really cares about the countryside and cares about farming.' But a local MP who, the article told readers, was once a Shadow Secretary of State for Wales, disagreed. I had heard of the politician, but did not know that he ever had anything to do with Wales – even remotely, which showed either my ignorance, or how ineffectual he was. The MP went on to say things like 'Welsh public services are in a perilous state and might drag Herefordshire down', and 'there are tremendous cultural links on both sides of the border and we should be celebrating that, rather than moving it.'

His statement finished on what he obviously intended to be a light-hearted note, but I found a bit puzzling. 'King Offa would be turning in his grave at the thought of moving the border anywhere other than on his Dyke!' Think about it.

The response to the 'Hereford in Wales?' question was not as straightforward as I thought it might be. Surprisingly, some English posters said it would be a good idea from a practical point of view, 'free prescriptions, think ahead!' ... 'maybe the council tax would be cheaper! It's at least £400 more expensive than it is in Powys.'

Many expressed their frustration with the current position, 'we deserve a better service from our government – if they can't help maybe it would be better for Hereford to be part of Wales – most English people already think we live in Wales – I'm all for it, we'll get better roads etc.'

But not everyone agreed ...

'No, no, no – outrageous, nonsensical, absurd, Herefordshire has been a part of the Kingdom of England since at least 927AD and before that, part of the English Kingdom of Mercia. What a ridiculous idea!'

And others were in favour of a swap ...

'Give the English back Monmouthshire and Pembrokeshire (little England beyond Wales) and you have a deal.'

After a while, it all got a bit confusing. Someone with a name so Welsh it might have been hewn from a quarry in Blaenau Ffestiniog said, 'Awful idea. People fought and built walls to keep the Welsh out. English till I die.'

Other posters clouded the issue even further. A 'Welshman in exile' wrote, 'whatever you do, don't allow Hereford to become part of the bleak, corrupt, mediocre and poverty-hit disgrace that is modern Wales.'

Yet another point of view was expressed by someone, presumably English, who having said that 'Herefordshire was never totally conquered and thus was never part of Anglo-Saxon England', invited anyone with a Welsh surname living in Herefordshire 'to take a quick look at their family history' where they will 'find that your family isn't as 'English' as you may think! The border as we know it today was only created afterwards! Wales for ever!'

A few people seemed to think that the county should be split up, with the land to the west of the A49 being ceded to Wales and a big chunk to the east going to Worcestershire. I went to bed thinking that nationalism was more complicated than I had thought it was going to be. I got up, thought about it some more, and realised it was even more complicated than that.

I was getting better at starting conversations with likely-looking people. More often than not, a simple question asking if I was listening to a local accent did the trick. The next morning, I went into a corner shop, bought a newspaper and asked the young couple serving if they were from Hereford. They were. In between customers, we talked about the changing town and changing times. Their answers were good-humoured, perceptive and helped give me another view of the place. If you think the exchanges sound a bit disjointed, you are right, but people had to make a living and customers had to be served. Was it true that no-one born and brought up in Hereford pronounced the first 'H' when they were speaking about the town?

They both smiled. The man was the first to answer. Still with a little smile on his face he said, 'Probably, well sort of.'

As a punk came in for his tobacco and papers, the woman tried to clarify the matter. 'It's not 'ereford, more *yurford*.' Apologies for any phonetic spelling mistakes, but I am new to all this.

Had they heard of the call to 'transfer' parts of the county to Wales? They had not, but were not totally surprised. Why?

'Because we're forgotten about, I suppose. No-one in government gives a toss about us – the roads are rubbish ...'

The woman did not want to be left out. 'The trains are rubbish.'

She smiled and added more. 'The rubbish's rubbish – separate this, separate that – recycle, bottles in here cans in there ... '

The man started getting agitated. 'I've heard a lot of it just gets buried together ... '

I could recognise a local government rant brewing and decided it was time to tell them about my quest to find 'border' people.

'What are they?'

'Don't think there's any definition, but I suppose I mean people who aren't really Welsh or English.' The woman looked puzzled. 'You mean a mixture of both?' I was not sure, at least not in the sense I meant before I got on my first bus in Prestatyn.

'Perhaps I mean people who aren't bothered either way.'

This time it was the man's turn to ask a question. 'Met many like that?'

'A few, probably more than I thought.'

Two young plump children came in for their breakfast of smokey bacon crisps and I knew I needed to get back to Hereford. Was it a border town?

'Don't know about that, but it's a lively town on the weekends, isn't that right?' The woman agreed. 'Very cheap booze – lots of drinking.'

'You don't see many people our age in some bits of town at night.'

I remembered what an old friend (who used to be known as the 'Mayor of Gresford') had once told me about Wrexham. 'It's always been a bit rough, bound to be when you think about it, surrounded by big villages that don't get on – pits, steel, a barracks and it's a *border* town. Border towns are usually lively old places!'

It was time to thank my helpful shop keepers and head for the bus station. As I walked along a litter-free road, I remembered a few lines from a spoof poem, *Hell in Herefordshire*, published in *Punch* a few years after the end of the First World War. Later I looked it up. It was written in the style of A. E. Houseman in response to the Bishop of Hereford's complaint about the amount of cider secretly brewed and drunk in the county. The second verse sums up a few of the problems caused by the cider harvest and the nature of society in the lands that stretch towards Offa's Dyke ...

> Unspeakable carouses that shame the summer sky
> Take place in little houses that look towards the Wye
> And near the Radnor border and the dark hill of Wales
> Beelzebub is warder and sorcery prevails

For some reason, the poem put me in an even better mood. Let it be recorded that I was even happy enough to smile at a saccharine sign on the back window of a car, 'Little Princess on board'; usually when I see signs like these I have an almost overwhelming urge to be sick.

The weather was beginning to break. The clear skies of the morning before had been replaced with thickening cloud that suggested that the thunderstorms promised by the weather people might turn up later today. As usual, the warnings were couched in apocalyptic terms – severe weather warning! Don't go out unless you have to! It could be the end of the world as we know it! Weather pros or weather birds just love standing like little battlefield generals in front of moving maps – all sweeping hand gestures, dramatic pauses and random emphases – look at me! I can do more than read the weather! I want my own chat show!

I strolled along to the country bus station enjoying the images conjured up by the name. Before my first trip, I had imagined trundling through leafy lanes on vehicles old enough to have seen service in the days when families could saunter around town centres at night, but of course I was to be wrong. The buses I had caught so far were sleek, modern beasts with enough acceleration to please a boy racer. Today's was no exception and the only difference was that it was a double-decker that was on its way to Cardiff, via Abergavenny and Tredegar. I chose downstairs and spent the journey talking to a nice, chatty Welsh couple who last year had celebrated their diamond wedding (sixty years for those like me who did not know) and had been visiting one of their daughters who lived in a village just outside Hereford. After a while, I told them that in at least some parts of the border, I had the impression that people looked across it and did not particularly like what they saw.

'That's not right,' the man shook his head in some sorrow. 'Can't be right, we should all get on.'

Then, as we left suburbs behind, I asked if they could think of any differences between Welsh and English people.

For a moment or two, the couple did some thinking before the woman told me that a Welsh host would always say to visitors, 'I'll put the kettle on', almost as soon as they crossed the threshold, but sometimes in England, 'you don't get offered anything, even if the people you're seeing are nice.'

Her husband agreed and invited me to do the same. 'Strange, isn't it?'

In the distance, I could see a fine mist of rain blurring blue-green hills as the pair started telling me more about their daughter who had lived in Herefordshire for many years and now worked on a part-time basis. How had she found the locals? Fine, no problem – everyone was friendly, great. As the driver switched on the windscreen wipers, I told them the people I had met so far had been the same. Then a tiny troubled frown appeared on the woman's face. 'But my daughter said that deep down, they don't *really* like the Welsh.'

'Why?'

'Don't know, it's just one of those things I suppose.'

Just after Pontrilas, an English village with a Welsh name, heavy rain began to batter the bus as if it was personal, but I could still see the start of the lovely little road I had once taken on the way to Hay-on-Wye to meet my sister. After catching up with family news, she had told me about a recent car journey she had made with a man who apparently said things like 'so I went into the bathroom, ran the cold tap, got my toothbrush from the beaker, held it in the water for a few seconds, took it out and squeezed some toothpaste on it, then cleaned my teeth, rinsed the brush then put it back, after that I washed my face with a blue flannel I keep on ... '

And he had kept on while she waited for a punch line that never came. It was perhaps ironic that she told me in a town where at certain times of the year, a local bylaw requires anyone opening their mouths to say something witty. I remembered the story and was glad that so far I had managed to avoid meeting the man with detailed knowledge of bathroom procedures who lived in the sodden countryside we were travelling through. Soon we reached a bridge over a river. It might or might not have been the Monnow, but it was definitely the border with Wales.

Across the aisle, the old couple attracted my attention and then told me that in the days when they still drove, every time they passed this point on their journey home they both cheered. For a second or so, I knew they were remembering times past. As we passed a sloping field that led up to an impressive stand of trees, the woman gave me a gentle, happy smile and said, 'Don't know why, but we always did.'

It was not long before I saw a sign that informed travellers they had arrived at the 'Gateway to Wales'. In this case, it was Abergavenny, but I had read the same description before. For those interested, Chepstow, Shrewsbury, Hereford, Leominster and Newport were also included in this select category. Which one is the real gateway? Don't you think we should be told? Couldn't someone come up with a different phrase? Does it matter?

Even in rain heavy enough to turn roads into shiny black, rippling streams, Abergavenny had a certain *something*. It had either grown since my last visit or those mischievous youthful memories were up to their old tricks. I said goodbye to my friends from valley Wales and headed for the Tourist Information Centre next to the bus station, cursing my last-minute decision to leave an umbrella behind. There are few sights more pitiful than a middle-aged writer (poetic licence) trying to recapture the speed and agility of a sporting youth so that he could dodge deep puddles on the way to shelter. Relentless rain stung my eyes as the downpour reached epic proportions while I thought that for once, the weather people had been right.

As I had come to expect, the well-stocked centre was staffed by friendly, helpful people. It was also busy with dripping tourists who thought of Sod's Law as they looked at brochures filled with pictures taken on bright sunny days where gloomy clouds are banned. In one corner, two women in their middle thirties, with short sensible hair, good- quality hiker's clothes and OS maps protected by purpose-made plastic, spoke quietly as they waited to get outside and walk. I wondered where they were going. After the pair exchanged slightly guarded looks, the one with ash-blonde hair said, 'We're doing a bit of the Offa's Dyke Path.'

I gestured enthusiastically towards windows now opaque with running water. 'Well, let's hope it clears up!'

Both women, faces as still as a gambler's, nodded agreement and one even managed a barely audible two word sentence. 'Hope so.'

'Have you walked any of it before?'

They glanced at each other, before the taller one gave a decisive answer. 'Yes.'

It was like pulling teeth, but after all, there was no statutory requirement for them to spend a few minutes passing the time of day with a stranger who decided to ask one more question. Where were they from?

In a surprisingly short time I was given an answer. 'Devon.'

For a moment, it seemed that the ash-blonde would add more, but then decided against it. In the slightly awkward silence, her friend muttered something in a tiny thin voice about walking the path over a period of years, then both moved a little closer to each other and the strange, somehow unsatisfactory encounter, was over. It was time to leave them to the comfort of their exclusive two-member club.

One of the staff told me where I would find the nearest café and I headed outside and found the downpour had become a deluge. Trying to tell myself that it was only water, I splashed through waves running down a little walled lane that led in the general direction of St Mary's Priory Church and the café that forms part of the adjoining Tithe Barn. Within minutes, I experienced the joyous feeling of having reached a warm, dry promised land in the shape of a superbly restored building, which was one of those lottery and publicly funded projects that seemed to be a good use of time and money, at least to one very damp visitor from Gower. The bilingual menu, based as it was on local produce, helped reinforce the image of a town in the middle of food riches – Black Mountain Smoked Haddock, Monmouthshire beef, Welsh grain mustard, local cheeses, local beers – local was the new organic. And if you can have locally-produced organic, start adding the pound signs. I might have missed something, but Hereford cider apple chutney appeared to be the sole representative from across the border to the east. Things had changed. In less than a decade, Abergavenny's Food Festival has become one of the best – at least in the opinions of some people paid to know these things – and given the competition from hundreds of others that have started in recent years, it has been a fair old achievement.

At nearby tables, diners chatted away quite happily in accents that ranged from southern England to southern Wales. All seemed happy to be here. Glancing outside, I shared their feelings. It was not just a wish to keep out of the rain that made me go upstairs and find out more about the barn, church and town. Honestly. Against one wall, a lovingly worked tapestry was meant to tell visitors all about the history of Abergavenny. It might well have done, but I was not one of the visitors who looked too closely. To me, tapestry has always been something worthy, but essentially dull – a bit like brownish wholemeal pasta – probably good for you, but you would not eat it from choice. In another part of the room, multimedia displays helped tell the story of the twelfth century building that had seen its fair share of changes over the years. I learned that after it finished being used to hold tithes or taxes, it branched out in new directions and at different periods in the last 900 years or so acted as a grain store, theatre and carpet warehouse before ending up as the scene of Abergavenny's first discotheque.

The displays were good, but the rain had nearly stopped and I wanted to look around the market town. Besides, history is all very well, but like those awful boasting round-robin letters at Christmas, there is only so much you can take at one time. I usually stop reading after the first paragraph, when people we have not seen for decades, tell us that adorable little six-year-old Daisy-Bunny, who is not just the brightest girl in her class, but in the whole known world, has been asked to sort out the problems of the Middle East in between making a film with Brad Pitt and touching up the ceiling on the Sistine Chapel.

Abergavenny might well be one of the many 'Gateways to Wales', yet it did not give the impression of being a border town. It was resolutely Welsh, from the accents of people I overheard in shops and streets to the contents of its local paper. For a happy hour or so, I wandered about and tried to get a feel for the place. In one shop, I asked a helpful young woman about the campaign to stop a big new supermarket being built on the edge of town and was once again struck by the strong emotions some people have for or against such developments. From what I saw and heard, a lot of energy is going into efforts to attract new independent shops or preserve those that are already there, so that Abergavenny's unique character is not lost under a welter of high-street names that might be found anywhere.

But all this walking and talking had made me thirsty; it was time for afternoon tea. In a quiet cafe opposite a well-stocked book shop, I sat down at a table, resolutely put away the *Western Mail* I had just bought, and prepared to write a few notes and draw the odd sketch or two about my visit so far. On the next table, a youngish man (I'm no good with ages) was reading a Welsh-language newspaper. Through the smeared lenses of my own, I noticed his spotless glasses, good-quality casual clothes and a face that suggested a sunny disposition. I sipped my tea, and tried to remember the conversations I'd had so far in this town that was, for the moment at least, still above water. It was not easy. My memory was fading away even faster than my bank balance. After shaking my head in frustration, I looked up to see the young man staring across at the few scribbles and doodles that represented a quarter of an hour's work. For some reason I felt the need to explain.

'Not making much progress.'

'Are you trying to write or draw?'

'Write mainly.'

'What?'

'A book, I suppose.'

He put down his paper, asked me what the book was about and in much less than a minute I had told him. By the time I reached the Severn near Sedbury, I hoped I would be able to shave off quite a bit more time and set a challenging personal best. If I did – well, even the thirty seconds barrier would be in range. We can all dream.

'Have you got a chapter on the Welsh language?' His accent was similar to that of an old friend who had grown up on Anglesey. When I told him I had not, he seemed disappointed, but it was still in a polite voice that he asked another question. 'Don't you think you should?'

'Not sure,' was shorthand for 'no'. 'It's not really like that, I just catch buses and chat to people – if things come up, I put them in.'

He might have said, 'Fine, fair enough,' but why did I feel it was not? Oh well – and then for the next few minutes, I told him about the trips I had taken so far.

'What's been your favourite?'

I might have said, 'Can't say yet, haven't done them all', but a possible winner came to mind.

'Very diplomatic.' We both smiled before he went back to language issues. 'What have people said about the Welsh language?'

'In Wales?'

'On both sides of the border. Have you asked them?'

My tea grew cold as we talked and then it was my turn to ask a final question that I could not really answer myself.

'What's it like being a Welsh speaker in Wales today?'

For a few seconds, he gave the matter due consideration. 'I suppose it's quite complicated, we know the language is meant to have legal status and parity and so on, but it's not that simple.'

'Why not?' Even as I asked the question, I knew it was never that simple, because things to do with nationality are rarely straightforward.

'Sometimes we spend too much time having to justify ourselves to non-Welsh speakers, even if they're Welsh themselves.'

'But surely not *all* non-Welsh speakers?'

'No, course not.' He did more thinking. 'And some English people who live here are great; lots of them are happy their children learn the language in school and some of them learn it themselves. It's just that ... ' and for a moment, there was silence as he struggled to choose the right words.

I tried to help out. 'Deep down you feel you shouldn't have to justify yourself at all, if you want to use Welsh you should be able to without worrying too much – is that right?'

'Yes, probably – it's a bit one-sided. No-one ever asks English speakers to justify or prove anything, do they?'

'Probably not.' I had enjoyed the conversation but it was time to have another look round before catching the bus back to Hereford.

'Time for me to go.' We both stood up and shook hands; it seemed the natural thing to do.

The rain had eased to a drizzle as I crossed the road to the indoor market which was quiet at this late stage of the afternoon. Markets usually tell you something about the town and the surrounding countryside, but this one offered few clues. Perhaps I was not sharp enough to find them. Perhaps it was time to head for the lane that led to the bus station.

The man in front of me was not really walking, but moving in a rather odd way. Every few seconds, he paused and then rotated his right arm a few times. I could not see his face, just his back. He wore a wet, blue tee-shirt, jeans and boots with Cuban heels. It was only when he stopped moving and started singing, I realised he was holding an invisible microphone. I knew the song. There had been lots of versions, but in my opinion, the Platters were way ahead of the field …

> Oh yes I'm the great pretender
> Pretending that I'm doing well
> My need is such I pretend too much
> I'm lonely but no-one can tell …

I stood a few yards behind him as he went into the chorus. I felt like joining in and for those who know the words, I bet you would have done so too …

> Too real is this feeling of make believe
> Too real when I feel what my heart can't conceal
> … ooh ooh

He must have sensed my presence and turned round to see me smiling. Judging by his thinning hair and lined face, I would say he heard the song when it first came out. He looked like a faded fifties pop star that time had not treated too well, but he had a decent voice and did not seem to be crazy. He smiled back and gestured towards the wall that ran down one side of the lane.

'The acoustics help.'

'I enjoyed it, it's one of my favourites.'

'And mine, thanks.'

We walked towards the bus station. I told him about a man I knew years ago in Wrexham who used to walk around supermarkets testing their acoustics with a couple of lines from Welsh hymns. No-one bothered him. He shopped, he sang, he paid. Maybe things were simpler then. Today, trained counsellors would get involved and a mild eccentricity would become a problem.

A few minutes later, we reached a parting of the ways. I was catching a bus. Frankie Fifties was going back to his car for the drive to a village I guessed was somewhere in the eastern valleys. We said goodbye and I stood near a little group of people and thought about Abergavenny. Next to me, a couple of seniors as we are encouraged to call them these days, were in the middle of an animated discussion about bargains. In less than five minutes, I had learned a lot more about offers available in and around the towns of Ebbw Vale and Tredegar. Then the woman turned around and got me involved.

'You'd never believe it, would you? Two paninis for the price of one – two!' The man was in before I could say anything. 'Never!'

'I'll show you.' It did not take long for the woman to root through her bag and show us a crumpled promotional flyer that confirmed that yes, two paninis could be bought for the price of one!

'See?' The woman had a contented look on her face as the audience marvelled at the offer. While the man told us about bargain breakfasts he had known, I wondered if the little episode revealed more generalised truths. So far every valley man or woman I had met had been very friendly and talkative, but was there a reason why someone coined the phrase 'land of the twitching curtain'? From bargains, we moved on to the weather. The man had to leave to catch his bus, but the woman did not break stride as she told me about a forthcoming eisteddfod to be held in Ebbw Vale which she hoped would not be spoiled by a downpour like today's. And then a pleased and proud expression came over her face as she asked me a question I had no chance of answering.

'Do you know who I met when I was a little girl?'

For understandable reasons, I hesitated, then mumbled, 'Umm no, afraid not.'

'Paul Robeson – I shook his hand as well – Paul Robeson.'

'That must have been fantastic.'

A wide grin took her back to childhood. 'It was, oh … there's my bus, 'bye.'

While I waited for mine, I ran through what I knew about the singer's links with Wales. It did not take long, but as the Hereford bus arrived, I had managed to put together a little mental map filled with images of miners, the struggles of organised labour, state-department politics and the bonds of affection that tied a world-famous figure to the tens of thousands of Welsh men and women who had to work for a living. More rain was falling as we joined a queue of traffic waiting at temporary lights. At least the delay gave me a chance to write down a few thoughts about the town I was about to leave, but within minutes, we were hammering down a wet road as if chased by the Hounds from Hell. For the first time ever on a bus, I wondered if I should wear the seat belt provided. It did not take too long to decide and by the time we had swept around a long right-handed bend, the belt was clicked in place and my face wore a slightly embarrassed look. Just across the aisle behind me, a voice said, 'Good idea.' I looked around to see a young woman following my lead.

She was from Nottingham, but now lived near Cardiff and was on her way to Hereford to stay with a friend for a couple of days. She was going by bus because her car was off the road. She had met her boyfriend at university in Newcastle. He was Welsh, but taught in a school in one of the Medway towns. I hope you are concentrating, because you will be tested later. It did not take long to ask this nice, but rather earnest young woman, if she considered herself to be English or British. 'Neither, I think I'm more European than anything else – my boyfriend feels the same way.'

Her answer surprised me. 'European? Why?'

She gave me a little smile and then listed a few reasons. 'Language, culture, economics, politics, the environment – those kinds of things – they're all really European, aren't they?

'Well they've all got a European dimension, but ... '

'Look, who're your favourite painters?'

'Monet, Cezanne, Pissarro, Picasso, Breughel – the usual crew, I suppose.'

Her brown eyes brightened in anticipation of proving a point and she could hardly wait to ask another question. 'What about composers?'

I thought for a moment. 'Let's see – Mozart, Beethoven, Verdi, Puccini, Mozart ... '

'You said him twice.'

It was my turn to smile. 'He's twice as good.' It was not too difficult to work out her strategy. 'Presumably you're going to tell me they're all European – right?'

'Yes, they're our heritage – our European heritage.'

We were passing an attractive red sandstone (my usual guess) pub which probably sold lager which might have been brewed anywhere between Burton and Budweiser – in beer terms, maybe she had a point.

'So your boyfriend feels the same?'

She nodded. 'Yes.'

'And he's Welsh ... '

'Yes, from Carmarthen.' There was a silence for a few seconds while I did some thinking. Just as we passed the sign welcoming us to Herefordshire and England, she spoke again.

'I suppose that's why we get on – we've got a lot in common.'

'Of course.'

I might have sounded like a sympathetic counsellor, but as I did not want her going into lurid details about their compatibility, I moved on to less problematic topics of conversation. By the time we reached Hereford bus station, we had discussed whether men and women had a different sense of humour, and were wondering if there was anyone, anywhere, who laughed at clowns. When the bus stopped, we got off along with the remaining six or seven passengers. She was going to meet her friend and I was going to sit down and try to get my thoughts together about the Hereford to Abergavenny leg of my journey. It was not easy – after all, I had read the strong views of English patriots with names that could have come from a Welsh-language soap opera, been soaked by a deluge of biblical proportions, met two women from Devon who wished they had never met me, been flung around a speeding bus, been made to feel guilty for not including a chapter devoted to the Welsh language, and was still shocked from hearing about a young man who had decided to change his nationality from Welsh to European.

But overall it had not been too bad. I had spoken to polite, friendly people, heard one of my favourite songs sung by an engaging eccentric, looked at buildings attractive enough to lift the spirits, been reminded that while issues associated with nationality were complex, they were also very interesting and despite the rain, had seen some lovely countryside. My mind was confused, perhaps a drink would help. After all, I was in Hereford, had not tasted cider for years and there was a pub not far away across the road ...

The bar was more crowded than I had expected. It looked like the kind of place where smokers would be in a majority if the law allowed them to puff away as they talked to their friends and enjoyed a pint or two. It was not a chintzy *ye olde pubbe*, or a gastro-pub which had yards of unread books as wallpaper, it was just a pub. As I waited to be served, I listened to snatches of conversations. Most of them seemed to be based on local people and places, rather than abstract ideas. International topics, with the exception of the wars in Iraq and Afghanistan, seemed to be almost non-existent. With a healthy-looking pint, I sat down and turned to the sports pages of the *Western Mail*.

On the next table, two old friends laughed and joked about someone they both knew. Their humour seemed to be gentle and affectionate, rather than savage and malicious. I read, half listened and relaxed. One of the cheerful pair went to buy his round; his slimmer friend who wore unexpectedly stylish glasses, asked me a question.

'What's your team – Cardiff City?'

'Afraid not, what makes you think it is?'

He gave me a little knowing smile and pointed. 'Because it's a Cardiff paper!'

'Well not just Cardiff. They sell it all over.'

'But mainly in south Wales.'

'Yes, that's probably right.'

'You still haven't told me your team.'

My brain was tired from a day's thinking, but at least I had not been asked a difficult question.

'Wrexham for football, the Ospreys for rugby – it used to be Swansea before they joined with Neath and everything changed.'

His friend came back with the beers and heard the last part of the conversation.

'Why Wrexham?'

'My sons started going to matches and I suppose I followed.'

They were Hereford fans and for a few minutes we spoke about the history and changing fortunes of football teams, including the nonsense of deducting league points because of the behaviour and private life of chairmen and directors. One of them asked me if I knew that Hereford had won the Welsh Cup in the days when English teams along the border were allowed to compete.

'No, I didn't know that, but I remember Shrewsbury and Chester either getting to the final or winning it.'

The more comfortably built one smiled. 'And do you know who we beat in the final? Have a guess.'

It had to be Wrexham. It was. Groan. Now that some form of good relations had been established, I asked the two if they had any thoughts about Wales and the Welsh. They both looked a little puzzled.

'What do you mean?' This time it was the slim one.

As pub conversations continued all around us, I gave them a potted history of my reasons for trying to write 'Offa', and what I had found on my journey so far. I gave them an encouraging smile and said it was their chance to see themselves in print. They said they understood and if I thought what they had to say might help – I paraphrase the comments and questions of two perceptive and thoughtful men, at least one of whom had probably left school at the first chance he had, 'because I didn't really like learning at the time.'

Both of them thought that Wales was a very different place, probably something to do with the language. Even if the majority were not fluent Welsh speakers? Yes, because language was more than knowing how to say something, it was a way of thinking about things – about who you were, where you fitted in, what others thought about you, what you thought about yourself. Both felt that most Welsh men and women were sensitive, prickly, emotional, quick to take offence and quick to forget it afterwards. Wales was an easy place to get to, but a hard place to get to know.

Did they think there were 'border' people? Not really, although people living in little rural communities in both countries shared the same problems that mainly stemmed from the inability of city-based politicians to understand the countryside. After they had run out of steam, I asked them if they liked the Welsh. They both hesitated, before telling me that they usually liked the individual, but collectively – yes, collectively they were not so sure. I stood up

and offered to buy them another drink. The slim one winked at his friend, then both looked across at me and pushed their empty glasses in my direction.

'I've always said the Welsh are very generous people. That's right isn't it?'

His comfortable friend agreed. 'Hardly a day goes by when you don't tell me that.'

He smiled. 'Best bitter please.'

Ross-on-Wye to Monmouth

A S EXPECTED, the sun broke through early clouds to welcome me to the picturesque Herefordshire town of Ross-on- Wye. I would have found it surprising if it had not, because to me, the lands that border the Severn and Wye will be forever sunlit. For those reading these words in the same border country as torrential rain falls from pewter skies, I can only offer my humble apologies. I am truly sorry, but I can only write as I find, and every time I have been to this particular part of these islands, sunshine has followed me around like a spotlight on a stage. Today was no exception. And so, on the afternoon before I caught a bus to neighbouring Monmouth, I walked through Ross-on-Wye in temperatures hot enough to make a bushman feel at home.

But in one sense today was exceptional, I was walking with a purpose; I was following my first ever town trail. I had picked up the leaflet in a bright and cheerful tourist office, packed with visitors from all over, and headed for the seventeenth century Market House where I planned to start and finish my tour. A few hours later, I knew at least a little bit more about this lovely market town. My research might have been superficial, but let no-one be alarmed, I am never going to become the official historian for Ross-on-Wye. As is usual in such matters, a number of famous historical figures had spent time in the place – even if was only for the night – including Walter Scott, George IV, Nelson and Sir Frederick Burrows. Who? You know, *the* Sir Frederick Burrows, the one who started working life as a railway porter, but ended it as the last Governor of Bengal. Do not worry, I had never heard of him either.

My first fleeting visit to Ross had been made many years ago, at the end of a bitterly cold, but beautifully sunny, winter's day. It was like one of those days promised by expensive hotels when they try and sell you a relaxing weekend break based on country walks, fresh air, good food, wood fires, reviving drinks and the hint of more sex than usual. I remembered an afternoon closing in as a friend drove us back to Swansea. We had started feeling hungry after Birmingham and by the time we saw the impressive spire of St Mary's church in the distance, lamp-lit Ross-on-Wye looked to be the kind of welcoming place where we might find some good food. It was. My memories were of hot soup, decent rolls and an open fire in a pub filled with pleasant low-key locals. Today, that combination would have made me run through the town flinging my clothes away as I headed for a cooling swim in the Wye. I was feeling as hot now as I had felt cold then. By the time I reached the riverside Rope Walk, I needed to sit down, sip from the warm dregs of a plastic bottle of water I found in my rucksack and decide if I was going to cut a few corners on my way back to the Market House.

My trail brochure told me that in 1802, Nelson and his party of guests took a pleasure boat to Monmouth from near this very spot. I thought back to that July day some two hundred years ago and wondered if Nelson and his party were as hot and thirsty then as I was now, or if the river they used was as clear and placid as it seemed to be today. We will probably never know – but I'd had enough history to be going on with; it was time to find an ice lolly and decide what to do.

On the first floor of a two-storey sandstone building, the Market House Heritage Centre was filled with interesting and slightly idiosyncratically chosen items and displays – from a 500 lbs German Second World War bomb which had landed in the grounds of a local hotel to big, black and white photographs of characters like rat catchers and drovers, who a century and more ago, could be seen around the town. I liked the centre on sight. It looked loved, used and useful. After a few minutes of pottering about, I spoke to a helpful woman who worked there. After agreeing that Ross had many charms, she told me she had been born and brought up in the town, although later had moved away through domestic circumstances. I asked her what its people were like.

'Well, independent for a start.' I did not respond, but waited for more explanation which duly came.

'Because of our history, I suppose.' She pointed to a display and poster on the opposite wall. 'This used to be called *Ergyn* or Archenfeld – the land of the Hedgehog – you see lots of hedgehogs on things round here.'

I dredged up a scrap of history. 'It wasn't really Welsh or English was it?'

'That's right, people could choose to pay taxes to a Welsh prince or English king or whatever.'

'But that was a long time ago. Does it really still affect the way people think about things?'

'Yes, it was sort of autonomous so ... '

'People got used to making more of their own decisions?'

She thought for a moment. 'Probably, I think it made them more independent minded anyway.'

'And feelings like these can be passed down through the centuries?'

'Why not?'

'Why not indeed.'

For someone writing a book about border attitudes and perceptions, this part of the country, with its ambivalent history, represented riches beyond compare. Perhaps you might consider the last phrase to be a little over the top and you might well be right, but I knew that later I needed to phone a friend to learn a bit more about *Ergyn*, Archenfeld, the Land of Hedgehogs or whatever it was called.

Soon we were joined by one of her male colleagues, a 'man of Ross' if that is the correct term. I asked them both if they felt English, British or something else. The woman was the first to answer, telling me it was probably British or maybe English. She was not really sure. Her colleague took quite a different approach and one that I had not come across on my journey so far. After considering the matter for a few seconds, he told us his first loyalty was to his family, then friends, then people who lived in his road, followed by those who lived in Ross-on-Wye. As far as he was concerned, nationality was less important than these personal ties. I asked him about local links with Wales.

'My daughter lives in Monmouth now, so I go there a lot.'

He went on to tell us about his daughter and her friend. Both were from Ross, but had lived in Monmouth for a while. Both were pregnant, but because his daughter wanted her baby to be born in Hereford, her local GP and surgery did not want to know. In contrast, her friend had been given much more help after she decided to have her baby in Wales. I did not quite know what to say, but wondered if he would have the same reaction if it had been the other way round and a Welsh girl from Monmouth, but now living in Ross, had chosen to have her baby in Newport. But he seemed a decent, fair-minded man, and I suspect he would have taken up cudgels on the girl's behalf. After a few quick words with his colleague, the man left.

As there were now only a handful of visitors in the place, I took the chance to ask about local accents. Were there any?

'Yes, of course, but I can't always pick them.' For a moment she thought some more and then said, 'I can tell south Herefordshire from north Herefordshire.'

'Could you tell if someone's from Gloucester?'

She hesitated, 'Probably.'

'Bristol?'

This time there was no hesitation. 'Definitely!'

'What about someone from Wales?'

'Oh yes, usually anyway – my daughter lives near Cardiff.'

For a few minutes we chatted about the differences, if any, between the two countries, but she probably had lots to do, so after thanking her, I left. Outside, a clutch of polite teenagers sat on some steps as a late afternoon drifted away in sunshine that picked out tiny motes of dust stirred up by a constant stream of modern cars passing the ancient building at the heart of their town. I found a quiet spot on a nearby street and phoned Andrew, a Welsh-speaking friend, who told me more about the complex history of this bit of border country. Apparently the peculiarly Welsh nature of these parts was acknowledged as early as the Domesday Book and that *Euas* (Ewyas) to the north and *Ergyn* or Archenfeld – the area around Ross, were called '*dwy wir lawes Gwent*', or the 'two true sleeves of Gwent'. They might have been 'thoroughly Welsh', but following their sixteenth-century incorporation within Herefordshire, this identity began to wane. Apparently, despite this gradual change, Elizabeth I felt Archenfeld was still Welsh enough to charge the Bishop of Hereford, together with the four bishops of Wales, with the translation of the Bible and the Book of Common Prayer into the language.

Against a background noise of bickering children who seemed to be fluent in Anglo Saxon, I was told that as late as the 1860s, many church warden notices, posted in local Herefordshire parishes, were bilingual. I found this hard to believe, but as my source is an honourable man, I pass it on for what it is worth. Why did all this come about? Andrew thought for a few seconds and then gave his opinion.

'I think Offa's Dyke was more a demarcation line than a defensive earthwork and that the break in the dyke in *Ergyn* or Archenfeld was there for a reason.'

'What sort of reason?'

'I think it was some kind of neutral territory, most of the people who lived there were Welsh, but they lived under a form of Mercian control – got all that?'

'Think so.'

'Good, what are you going to do tonight?'

'Get something to eat and have a pint.'

He laughed and said, 'That makes a change', before adding that while it was always interesting talking to me – I understood. 'You'd better get back to work then!' Some people are so conscientious.

An hour or so later, I sat down with a welcome beer outside a pub called *The Man of Ross* in the town centre and looked up to read some lines written on the white painted wall,

John Kyrle (1637–1724) local benefactor
He helped settle disputes, aided the poor and sick
Supported schools and left the Beautiful 'Prospect' walk with a fountain
for the citizens of Ross.

Whoever wrote it was right; the prospect was beautiful. I did not know about the rest, but it seemed the Man of Ross was a good man. I was still deciding how I would like to be remembered when a couple, who might have been in their early thirties, sat down at the next table. She was drinking lager, he was drinking lemonade. It was only fair; it was his turn to drive. I watched and wondered what John Kyrle would have made of it all. They saw me looking up at the lines and writing them down on my black notepad. They might both have wondered what I was doing, but she was the one to ask. I went through my well-practised spiel, but the heat of the day had taken its toll and I was nowhere near my average time for the trip so far.

'So you'll put that in your book?' It was her again.

'Don't know yet, but yes, probably – I'll do a bit of research and … '

Her husband broke in. 'Sorry, don't think we can tell you much about him.'

She looked affronted. 'Well *you* might not be able to, but I can.' He looked apprehensive, but stayed silent. I looked at her and waited, pen poised.

'Yes, well, he did lots for this place, lots of things – uh, they even named a street after him.'

For a few seconds she said nothing, but from her frown of concentration, some elusive facts were proving difficult to land. Then, with a sense of theatre, she pointed in the general direction of St Mary's and spoke. 'He's buried in the church yard. I think he gave them a bell.' The woman sat back with a smile of triumph and downed half her lager, before turning to her husband. 'See? Told you I knew something about him!'

To help keep the peace, I thanked her and changed the subject.

'Do you have any strong views either way about Wales?'

While he thought and sipped his lemonade, she said, 'Don't think Welsh people like us very much so I don't like them, present company excepted.'

I nodded in grateful thanks for her graceful compliment. 'Why do you think they don't like you?'

'I don't really know, but I'm sure it's true.' She turned to her husband for confirmation. 'I'm right, aren't I?'

He hesitated, and then went for it. 'Don't agree – most of them are OK, but you always get some, don't you?'

Judging by his wife's face, if he had any thoughts about a night of passion it would not be with the woman who sat opposite him. I decided to leave him to her tender mercies. If I had been in his position I would have gone for the odd few beers, a curry and the taxi home option. What did he have to lose? However, my new found maturity prevented me from giving him this piece of advice, so I simply thanked them both and walked away into the darkening night.

The bus to Monmouth left on time. The morning was bright with the promise of yet another sunny day to come and we passed small groups of cheerful people chatting away and appearing to find that life was worth living in this far corner of Herefordshire that seemed forever England. Next to a window, I sat alone, half turned inwards in an attempt to wedge myself more securely so that later, my notes might have a chance of being deciphered without having to call in the great Champollion. Anyone looking at some of the notes I had scribbled on a couple of the jolting trips I had made so far, would be forgiven for thinking I had been at the tequila since sunrise.

As was so often the case, we had a polite and helpful driver. Service seemed to still matter in many of the places I had visited so far and the big city high-street world of shop assistants who hold out a hand for your money while they talk about their grimy social lives seemed far away. Looking back on the sentence, I think I might have slipped back into my grumpy-old-man persona which just will not do on a morning as nice as this. Our little bus seemed to take random turnings as it meandered around some narrow country roads. We picked up and dropped off passengers while passing through countryside which could have starred in a Hollywood film about rural Britain. It was time to sit back, leave things to the driver and think about a conversation I had the night before.

Those paying attention would know that I had walked away into a darkening night after talking to a young couple about their views on Wales and the Welsh, but they would be forgiven for not knowing that a little later, I had spoken to a middle-aged man with a thin, intelligent face, leaning against the bar in another quiet town-centre pub, who had seen me looking at a brochure *Herefordshire Festivals and Events 2009*. I had been reading details of a workshop aimed at children aged eight years+ called *Woolly Wonders*, and wondered how many would actually turn up to try their hand at 'felting, spinning and knitting'. Judging by most of the families and children I knew, course tutors were highly likely to be spending their day playing solitaire, but maybe I was moving in the wrong circles.

I looked across at my thin-faced friend and said, 'There's a lot on.'

The man agreed in a pleasant, educated voice. Within minutes he was sitting at my table talking about the recent massive growth in organised leisure events held up and down the country. We seemed to agree on most things – leisure used to be free form, now it had structure – festivals have become specialised and are big business. As one pint became two, we spoke about the growth in specialist events. It did not take long for an element of competition to emerge. I had led off with a Glen Miller festival held in the south of England.

'Where?'

'Not sure, maybe Bedford.'

He had come back with kite festivals and a National Quince Day celebrated in the West Country. With some confidence, I told him about Festivals of Quilts and even, wait for it, an event held for the dreaded town criers. Many people would have conceded defeat at that stage, but he fought back with what turned out to be the winner.

'In Devon, they run the international worm charming championships!'

I just stared. Defeat had been snatched from the complacent jaws of victory. It was time to change the subject.

'Why aren't there more obvious traces of Wales around here?'

He looked slightly puzzled. 'What do you mean?'

'Considering how close we are to the border, and the fact this part used to be sort of Welsh ... '

'Archenfeld – yes, I see what you're on about, but it was a long time ago.'

'But shouldn't some traces remain?'

'Maybe they do, maybe you just haven't seen them, you've only been here a few hours, haven't you?'

I hesitated for a while. I looked at a long-married couple busy ignoring each other at a table near the door, before agreeing that yes, today was my first proper day in Ross.

'Well, are there any traces?'

It was his turn to hesitate. 'A few obvious ones, lots of Welsh surnames', he smiled. 'like mine – my family came over from mid Wales – names of local villages ... '

'Such as?'

'Llangarron, Welsh Bicknor, Pencraig – and we get Welsh Water round here, but it's not just those kinds of things, it's ... '

This time the hesitation was longer. He frowned as he tried to find the right words.

'Well, could be something to do with an attitude of mind – in these parts some people feel we're a bit out of things, a bit of an afterthought.'

'Like the people in Wales?'

This time there was no pause. 'Yes, could be.'

It had been the jumping off point for a stimulating conversation that lasted until he wished me well with my book and headed past our long married couple still grimly spending quality time together as they tell you to do in the glossy magazines.

I had just finished thinking about advice given by lifestyle gurus when we pulled into Monmouth's cattle market car park and I wondered if there was still one (a market, not a car park in case you are confused). Monmouth, the birthplace of Henry V and Charles Rolls of fine car fame, appeared prosperous and confident enough not to tarnish its image through too much commercial exploitation of its history and I speak as a veteran of Fort William, where I was once offered a Rob Roy burger in a fast food joint. I smiled and nodded goodbye to my fellow travellers (once that would have raised eyebrows), and within minutes was looking in the windows of a chocolatier wondering if my New Year resolution would last. Within seconds I knew it would not and so, resolution shakily intact, I headed for the river – one of them at least (apparently Monmouth has three – the Monnow, Wye and Trothy), because a man can only stand so much temptation.

I had never seen anything quite like the bridge over the Monnow. This simple sentence does not begin to do justice to a lovely red sandstone (if that is what it was) structure that must have been at the heart of local events for over eight-hundred years, but it is the best I can come up with for now. It was lovely and so, in a gentle breeze that had blown over fields of sweet-smelling wild flowers, I moved closer to have a better look. For once, a giant Winnebago parked across three spaces failed to spoil my mood, but I still thought whoever was responsible was a selfish bastard. I paused for a second, considered an act of wanton vandalism involving a felt-tipped pen and some naughty words, before moving on trying not to think about the petty vanities of personalised number plates, but the effort was too much – what about BIG 1 – what a wit the owner must be! Or even DI4NE! Get it? My name is Diane and I have got MONEY!

As people walked their dogs on a bank-side path, a father and son threw little pieces of bread into the water and watched them drifting down in the current before being eaten by well-fed ducks that swam about in deeper pools and waited for their lunch to arrive. The dark-haired father looked like Rudolf Valentino's brother – the one who liked doughnuts. His skin-tight faded rugby jersey, which must have made breathing difficult, would have to stay on him until he lost weight and probably accounted for a strange throwing action that finished with a bent elbow, but walking over to the bilingual plaque that gave brief details of the structure's history, even this grumpy old man had the warming thought that father and son were at peace with the world and each other.

Apparently Monnow Bridge, which was built towards the end of the thirteenth century, is Britain's only surviving medieval bridge with a gate tower, but given that my knowledge of such things is pathetically limited, I

was happy to believe whoever was responsible for the research. I read that 'the gate house has served as toll house, guard room, gaol and dwelling house', which, at the very least, seems to show an admirable adaptability to changing circumstances over the centuries. I straightened up and said 'dwelling' a couple of times and felt even better for doing so. What a wonderful word – why don't we use it more often? It flowed from my lips without struggle and I said it again – dwelling. It was a word that brought back childhood images of good King Wenceslas and his page battling through deep snow towards a peasant's cottage as fat white flakes drifted down from an indigo sky, but that was a long time ago in a far away country.

In sharp contrast to the penetrating cold that must have affected the Kingdom of Wenceslas for most of the long, gloomy winter months, and with a bit of poetic licence, the bridge's stones were warm enough to bring back memories of summer holidays in southern France. For a few moments, I enjoyed just *being*, only vaguely aware of the relaxed conversations of locals as they passed me on their way to the centre of town, knowing that all too soon, it would be time to follow them and find out what they thought about living so close to the border. By the time I reached the halfway point of the main street, I knew that if Henry V was still alive and well, and walking around town with a woman, there is a fair chance she would have been wearing a pair of giant sunglasses, spangled with fake jewels, on the top of her head, even though the day was now bright enough for an operating theatre. Thinking about it, her jewels would probably have been real, but we will never know.

Outside a coffee shop, a man and woman came towards me. Both had a pair of sunglasses perched in its now traditional position, but there was a daring variation on show. The woman had gone that crucial one step further, because on her broad forehead, there was another pair of sunglasses! He was more conservative. His second pair were probably reading glasses, but I did not want to get close enough to ask him. As they passed, I heard the tail-end of an animated conversation and wondered if she was putting pressure on him to follow her lead. Two people wearing four pairs of glasses used for decoration only, could start a fashion trend. If it caught on, it would not be too long before people would be strolling around wearing enough glasses to look like a close up of a fly's head.

It was time for a coffee and a glance through my usual daily newspaper. The lead story was a roadside bomb that had brought about the deaths of two soldiers in Afghanistan. Just as I was glancing at the details, a portly, red-faced man on the next table gave voice to my own thoughts.

'Terrible business.' There was no need to ask what he meant.

'Yes.'

'Don't know where it's going to end.'

He paused for a few seconds while he thought things through, 'or if it will end.' I did not know how to reply, but just looked again at the smiling faces of those killed and hoped that somewhere they had found the peace their families would never know. At that moment, the harsh dry mountains of Afghanistan seemed a long, long way from the peaceful green hills of this south-east corner of Wales. It was time to have a proper look around the town.

After leaving the café, I wandered up and down the imposing street that linked Agincourt Square with Monnow Bridge at the bottom of a shallow hill. As usual, some of the shops suffered from apostrophe theft, but on a bright sunny day, why should anyone get too upset by a missing comma that had got above itself?

The number of Welsh titles in the window of a well-stocked book shop came as something of a surprise, given that the town is only a hop, skip and a jump away from England. Modern technology might have its detractors, but they would not include those people, like me, who enjoy reading books about local history, scenery, rivers, folk tales, coastlines and the like. Many of these titles are now produced using low-cost technology; in earlier days, they would probably have remained as hand-written or typed pages, gathering dust on a shelf somewhere, as the author tried, and generally failed, to interest a publisher who was either too busy or grand to take their call. Here endeth the sermon from a bitter, failed novelist ...

Not far from the bookshop, some work was being done on the outside of what I took to be an impressive town hall, which seemed to be covered by sheeting. I moved over to have a closer look and saw stencilled verses, sentences that were big enough to read and drawings of people wearing clothes that might have been around when Shakespeare was writing to make ends meet. One of the quotations reminded me of where we were.

> Hail Monmouth's sons whose noble deeds
> Resound from shore to shore
> Whose praises will be ever sung
> Till time shall be no more.

I did not know the verse, but details of its provenance had been added by someone with an understanding of the ignorance of people like me. Apparently, the words came from a traditional song, published in 1822 by one Samuel Etheridge who came from Newport. It was not the only quotation on view. I stood on the edge of a small group of people and saw some lines I had last read when the Beatles were taking America by storm, 'there is good men born at Monmouth.' In case you are wondering, the approved words were spoken by Fluellen, a Welsh captain when he compared Henry V with Alexander. It might have been the product of the decent weather, but I looked around and saw pleasant men and women chatting amicably in the sunshine and felt the words were in tune with the warm afternoon.

There was plenty of history about, but it did not smack you in the face unlike some places I had been to in the recent past. I stood next to a very tall man wearing the type of old, rough tweed jacket you do not see too often these days and read about the trial of Chartist leaders. The details were given on a temporary display board that had been erected for the benefit of the curious or those with time on their hands. Apparently, on New Year's Eve 1839, twelve prisoners were brought here to face the consequences of breaking the law of the land. Nine were acquitted, but John Frost, Zephaniah Williams and William Jones were condemned to be hanged, drawn and quartered, although later, the sentence was reduced to transportation to Van Diemen's Land. The men must have been relieved; hanging, drawing and quartering sounds so final, that a trip to the unknown island off Australia must have been like finding your terminal illness was a diagnostic mistake. I wandered off towards the museum, wondering what it must have been like to have lived through the struggles to bring about political change and a society free from the shackles of deference and rewards based on the accident of birth. If you were rich, it was probably a mixture of interest and apprehension. If you were poor, you were probably too busy trying to meet your basic needs to bother too much about annual parliaments and payment for MPs.

I did not get to the museum because hunger beat culture 1-0. Less than ten minutes after the final whistle, I was sitting on the grassy bank of the Monnow enjoying a very good sandwich and cool drink, when a smartly-dressed man and woman, who looked old enough to remember the test card, walked over and sat down a few yards away. It did not take long for him to glance towards me and say something.

'Nice place. First time we've been here.'

'Where are you from?' We always like to know; it is in our genes.

This time it was his well-coiffed wife who spoke.

'Blackpool, well Thornton actually.' She sounded as if it should mean something to me. In case it did not, her husband added more detail.

'It's at the northern end of Blackpool. The right end if you get my drift – Thornton Cleveleys.'

I might have met my first ten-bob snob of the trip, but this was getting confusing. Did they live in Thornton or Thornton Cleveleys? Did it matter? Then it was her turn again. 'Have you ever been there?'

Something stirred within a layer of muddy memories. 'Yes, a couple of times, years ago.'

'Do you mean you've been to Blackpool or Thornton Cleveleys?'

For a second or so I wondered where this conversation would end, before her husband prompted me.

'They're very different.'

'I know, so you told me – right, let me think – OK, a couple of times to Blackpool and once to Cleveleys.'

It was her turn again. 'Why did you go to Cleveleys?' I glanced towards the river and thought about what I had started.

'Dropping something off I think. It was a long time ago.'

They both looked doubtful – surely someone could remember why they went to Cleveleys? The man leant towards me. I could see that he prided himself on a good, error-free, wet shave.

'Can you remember where it was – Lanefield Drive, Aintree Road ... '

This had to be stopped as soon as possible before they drove me to do something unfortunate. Even if I had remembered, what good would it have done any of us? But while I was thinking about a strategy short of hurling them in the general direction of the river, the woman resumed the interrogation.

'Was it anywhere near Woodland Avenue? That's where we live, not on the actual avenue but a road off it. It's not far from the windmill.'

I stood up and glanced towards them. 'Doesn't ring a bell, sorry must be going.'

But before I could do so, the clean-shaven man wanted to tell me something. 'Did you know Thornton was mentioned in the Domesday Book?'

For a moment I tried to take in what he had just said. I had gone for years without hearing the words 'Domesday Book', but now I had heard them twice in less than twenty-four hours – I was still wondering about coincidences, when the woman asked me if I was Welsh.

'Yes, from Gower – it's near Swansea.'

Her husband seemed affronted. 'We know Gower. We've spent a lot of time in Wales, travelled all round it ...'

His wife broke in. 'Except for this bit, never been here before, but we've been going to Wales since the children were small.'

I sighed, sat down again, took out my black notebook and pen and prepared to ask a few questions. I started off with one of my usuals. What came to mind when someone mentioned Wales? As the man started to tell me about how the country had changed since they had first started visiting, his wife broke in with another question of her own.

'Why are you writing it down?'

So I told them all about my book and the man told me all about Wales.

'Do you mind if I'm candid?'

I gave him a little encouraging smile. 'Feel free.'

The man gathered his thoughts for a few seconds before launching into his analysis of my country.

'When someone mentions Wales, I think arguments – the Welsh love an argument.' He turned to his wife and appealed for support. 'That's right, isn't it?'

The well-groomed woman from Thornton Cleveleys looked at me and slowly nodded her head as if to warn me that more was to come.

'Yes, that's right – you know what he told me once when we were staying at a hotel in Pembrokeshire? Go on have a guess.' I stared at the woman. How could I possibly know?

She was impatient to tell me. 'The Welsh are like squabbling children, that's what he said – you did, didn't you?'

Her husband nodded in turn and agreed that he had spoken those very words, before looking back to me.

'Think about it – the valleys squabble with the rest of Wales – the south and the north don't like each other – people who live in the countryside don't like people who live in the towns … '

His wife reinforced the point, saying meaningfully, 'and vice versa', before handing back to her husband who finished off with a touch of relish.

'And Welsh speakers squabble with everyone who can't speak the language!'

He shook his head. 'Sorry, but that's the way it is.'

The man might have finished, but his wife had one more question to ask. 'Aren't you going to write it down?'

I tapped the side of my head. 'Later, it's in here for now.' It was a good moment to say a fond farewell and leave.

For the next half hour or so, I wandered around and did some thinking about two towns in two countries – Ross- on-Wye and Monmouth. Superficially at least, they appeared to have a lot in common. They both gave the impression that they were conservative small towns where traditions mattered and even if Ross had the slightly bigger population, there was not that much in it. Both were attractive and both attracted visitors. They shared the same river and although Ross is the only town within the Wye Valley's Area of Outstanding Natural Beauty, Monmouth is close enough to reach it in minutes. According to something I had read, the Ross-on-Wye hockey team trains and plays its home games in Monmouth, while the same main road that links them also provides their best link to the outside world. I was just trying to remember their political leanings when someone asked me for directions.

'Do you know if the museum's open today?'

He was short, fat and sixty. His short, fat and sixty something wife added an explanation. 'We were hoping to go. We like going to museums, we always have. Some people sit in pubs, we walk around museums!'

Shoulders touching, they stood next to each like bookends. They were not wearing identical sea-green polo shirts, but they were a close enough match to suggest their tastes ran in the same direction. They both spoke with rich, rural accents that could have been used to sell farmhouse cheeses. His hair was short and sensible, so was hers. They looked as if they had been married since birth.

'Sorry, don't know – I was going to go myself an hour or so ago, but something got in the way.'

Neither said anything, but both looked curious and I felt I had to give them an explanation. I smiled. 'I was hungry.' They smiled, they understood.

It was her turn to ask a question. 'Are you going to go now?'

'Not sure. I'll have a stroll up there and think about it – haven't got much time.'

Like three old pals we started walking, line abreast, in the general direction of the museum. It turned out they lived 'in the Forest, near Coleford.' Had I been there?

'No.' My answer did not seem to surprise them.

'But you're proper Welsh aren't you? I suppose it's a long way for you.' I wondered where 'proper Welsh' people lived. The man attempted to explain. 'In little villages in the mountains.' He turned to his wife and best friend before smiling and saying. 'In little villages with difficult names for people like us!'

Memories made her smile. 'Yes, proper Welsh they are.'

It was time to try and clarify something. 'But don't proper Welsh people live around here?'

As his wife nodded agreement, the man said, 'Not sure about that. Monmouth's not really Wales is it? Not *proper* Wales.'

'Why not? It's in Wales.'

'Only just.'

'Does that matter?'

For a moment, the fat man hesitated and I wondered as if he was thinking about pies he had known. But his answer proved his mind was on the matter in hand.

'Yes, I think it does – and they've got a Tory MP, everywhere else in Wales votes Labour!'

Besides him, his wife glowed with the pride of a woman whose husband knew things like that. I did some quick thinking – he was right about the local constituency at least, even if the rest was wrong. I had forgotten that in the last election, the Conservatives had won Monmouth, but did that alone really mean it was not properly Welsh? Of course it did not. I did some more thinking.

Tories were not confined to constituencies that nestled up against the border with England. I had known Welsh-speaking Conservatives who lived in little villages in the heart of the mountains, as well as people who voted Conservative in the valleys of south Wales where the Labour vote was weighed, rather than counted. I was not sure I was up to a protracted discussion about it all, so said nothing that might start one. Within a few minutes, the three of us were standing outside the museum. At least one of us was deciding whether to go inside.

I had been brought up on Hornblower and the museum held a famous collection of Nelson paraphernalia. On the other hand, the afternoon was still very warm and a long cool drink would go down well. I knew I would come back to Monmouth; the museum could wait for another day. My companions were in a hurry to start looking at whatever was on offer and said their goodbyes with their minds already focused on the treasures they were about to see.

The return journey to Ross gave me just enough time to look back on the nine trips I had made since my starting point in a very cold Prestatyn. Had I learned much about the people who lived on either side of Offa's Dyke? Could any broad conclusions be drawn from what I had seen and heard so far?

As we neared the town, I hazily remembered George Borrow's *Wild Wales* and a piece of folklore quoted by the author. It went along the lines of 'it was customary for the English to cut off the ears of every Welshman found to the east of the dyke and for the Welsh to hang every Englishman they found to the west of it.' Well so far I had not met any deaf Welshmen in places like Chester, Shrewsbury, Leominster or Hereford nor seen any Englishmen dangling in the winds that blew over Welsh mountains, so perhaps things had changed with the centuries. But, as Mao Tse Tung had once said when asked about the lessons that might be drawn from the French Revolution, 'it's too soon to say.'

I got off the bus in Ross and nodded appreciation to yet another pleasant driver, just as another question came into my mind. I had yet to decide if my last journey – the leg between Chepstow and Sedbury on the Beachley peninsula, should include a walk to the southernmost point of the Offa's Dyke path.

As usual, there were arguments for and against, but perhaps they could wait for another time. Besides, didn't another great figure from Chinese history, Charlie Chan, once tell us that 'too much thinking and not enough drinking is bad for your health?' No? I could be wrong, but whoever said it, the advice had a compelling logic after a long, hot day on the banks of the Wye.

Chepstow to Sedbury

The last trip was also going to be my shortest. Barely three miles separate the Monmouthshire town of Chepstow from the Gloucestershire village of Sedbury, which lies on the Beachley Peninsula that separates the rivers Wye and Severn, and is close enough to one of the most easterly towns in Wales to be called a suburb.

My plans were in place and this time it should be easy. It would be a ten-minute bus ride to Sedbury, followed by a gentle stroll to my final destination – the spot on the northern bank of the River Severn which marks the southern end of the long-distance footpath named after the man who had ordered a dyke to be built between Wales and England – Mercia's very own King Offa. But before I caught that bus, I was going to buy some supplies and have a look around a town that some strangers hazily place in Wales or is it England – not sure, but it is on the border anyway. There is a castle there, on the river – the Wye, or it could be the Severn – not sure. Chepstow, give me a minute and I will remember …

Despite the noise and bustle of the supermarket, I had no trouble hearing the married couple who stood in front of me as we waited to pay at the checkout. It is not that I particularly wanted to listen to their conversation, but their penetrating voices gave me no other choice. The sandy-haired woman with the slightly blotchy face pointed to one of the bars of chocolate on the conveyor belt.

'When did they change the packet?'

She did not sound local, but I was not either, so I would not have bet my

Wales Grand Slam memorabilia on being correct. The man, knowing he needed to get it spot on, took a few seconds to answer. I listened, knowing that chocolate played an important part in their weekly rituals of domestic life.

'Think it was last January.'

The woman nodded in agreement.

'Think you're right.'

The man nodded in contentment.

'I am.'

A respectful distance behind them, I nodded in admiration. The knowledge some individuals have at their fingertips made me feel very humble. At the head of the queue, a young mother with a toddler daughter wearing pink everything, took a minute or so to find her purse while I wondered why actually having to pay for their purchases seemed to come as a surprise to some people. I was a veteran of standing in line at supermarket checkouts listening to shoppers telling their life stories to bored cashiers or checkout operatives as they are probably called these days. This morning's encounter was nothing out of the ordinary.

'What did you say, twenty-two pounds eighty one? Oh yes, sorry – where's my money, thought I had it here – Carly babes, stop doing that, she's not even five yet, can't believe it sometimes. Everyone says how clever she is, she can play a DVD and everything ... '

As a great philosopher of our time once said, 'unless they're family, other people's children are hell.'

Just after Carly babes' mother finally paid, and the little girl with adorable blonde curls and discreet eyeliner had told us that she wanted to be famous 'just like people on television' (cue smiles all round except from me), the man in front of me asked his wife a tricky question.

'I was thinking about it the other day – when did they change the name from Marathon to Snickers?'

She thought for a long moment, and then answered. '1990, I think.'

After some thought, he accepted her answer. 'Think you're right.'

This time it was her turn to nod in contentment. 'I am.'

It was a depressing thought to think that in this attractive town steeped in historical riches, at least one couple appeared to spend their waking hours thinking and talking about chocolate wrappers. But as I said in an earlier chapter, we all have our hobbies.

Outside, Saturday-morning Chepstow bustled about its business. I did not have to hurry, because the timetable suggested (gulp), that the bus service to Beachley via Sedbury was pretty good.

Within yards of the war memorial, which was sited half-way up the hill that led down to the river, I sat on warm stone steps and looked at a big gun, taken from a First World War German submarine, which appeared to be aimed in the general direction of Gloucestershire. According to an information board, it had been presented to the town by George V in recognition of the VC, posthumously awarded to Able Seaman William Charles Williams, who had been brought up in Chepstow, for the bravery he had shown during the Gallipoli campaign. Apparently, Williams had clung onto a rope which held lighters in place, so that our troops could disembark onto a landing beach from the SS *River Clyde*. In the midst of a hail of incoming enemy fire, he had stood chest deep in the sea for over an hour until one shell inflicted a fatal wound. It was hard to take in what it must have been like on that April morning in 1915, as death and destruction was unleashed on men who had been born or brought up in peaceful places like the Chepstow of today. After a few minutes thinking of complex issues I usually shied away from, I stood up to have a closer look at some of the names of soldiers, sailors and airmen who had died in two wars.

Able Seaman Williams was there of course, together with other young men I assumed had links with Chepstow and the surrounding area. I looked more closely at the details and saw the names of those who never again knew a sunny morning like this when soft winds brushed the sides of their neat, clean war memorial. To my right, slow-moving traffic made it easy for three teenage boys to cross the road. They were probably about the same age as many of those chosen by blind chance to die for their country or whatever cause they thought it to be. I watched and remembered my father once telling me that 'war isn't glamorous, it's dirty and dangerous – people don't just get flesh wounds and live happily ever after – they die from wounds I hope you never have to see.'

It was time to have a final look at the names. What a waste of young lives. I was still thinking of the injustice of it all when someone spoke to me.

'Excuse me, you got the time?'

A yard or so away, a deep-chested man was shaking a dodgy watch. I wondered why I had not noticed him arrive and then came to the conclusion it must either have been when I was distracted by the teenagers or he was a feather- footed Comanche scout.

'This is always giving me bloody problems.'

'Just gone half nine.'

'Thanks.'

His face looked a little lived in. He was not a dandy, but his clothes said money. His accent told me he probably was not a Comanche but came from somewhere west of the Loughor River that helps keep a barrier between Swansea Jacks and the good people of Llanelli. I was right; he might have lived in London for nearly forty years, but he was a Turk from greying hair to shiny shoes. Within ten minutes, I knew he had been born in Llanelli, had played rugby for Llanelli Grammar School, had parents who used to run a pub where regulars had sounded like the cast of *Under Milk Wood*, and then, after getting a maths degree from a Welsh university, had moved to London where he had worked and lived for nearly forty years. For a moment or two, he chatted about changes he had seen in London in an accent which was strong enough to suggest he had never crossed the Loughor Bridge, let alone Offa's Dyke. What was he doing in Chepstow? Considering he had already told me a lot in a little time, I was a bit taken aback by his vague answer that might have come from a novel about Cold War spies. Substitute Checkpoint Charlie for the bridge over the Wye and you get the picture. Then it was my turn to be quizzed.

'What's a Swansea Jack doing here?'

It did not take long to tell him about my book, because at this stage of my journey I was as slick as a salesman. When I had finished, he sat down next to me and started talking about language issues. It turned out that although he knew 'lots of words and phrases', he would not really call himself a Welsh speaker.

'It's not that easy. Take Welsh in schools – lots of English-speaking parents don't like it being taught at whatever level.'

'Do you mean English people?'

'Yes, and Welsh people who don't speak Welsh.'

'Why do you think they don't like it?'

He thought for a few seconds. 'Well, some of them don't think it should be compulsory and others say they'd rather their children learn a useful language, like French or Spanish or something – to help them get a job and all that.' As he was finishing his sentence, I thought back to a conversation I had once had with a woman who had spent many years teaching French and German in a secondary school. I had asked about the foreign-language skills of a typical sixteen-year-old school leaver and was told that given no learning difficulties or real problems at home, most would end up with some sort of GCSE grade, a smattering of vocabulary and the ability to ask for directions, say 'please' and 'thank you' and count to ten – provided that they were not trying to learn in a blackboard jungle. Better schools, with better teaching, usually meant a good GCSE, bigger vocabulary and a very limited ability to be understood in a foreign language. This ability would last for a few years at least, after which apparently, proficiency ebbs away through lack of use. She had finished up by telling me that unless you were talking about gifted, motivated students studying at post 'A' level standard, the teaching of foreign languages is not an educational success story.

It was time to get back to my new friend from the west. 'So you don't think GCSE French is going to help them get a job.'

'Where – in France?'

He was scornful. 'Course not, they would be better off concentrating on Welsh!'

'Because?'

'Because most school leavers in Wales end up staying in Wales.'

'Where they can hear Welsh everyday if they want to … '

'Yes, or watch S4C or listen to Radio Cymru or read newspapers – at least it's contact with the language isn't it?'

There was a moment's hesitation before he spoke again. 'If I had my way, only a few children would be allowed to learn foreign languages, the rest would be given double Welsh. If they are reasonably fluent, they've got more chance of getting a job in the country they'll probably live in – Wales!'

'Strong views.'

He smiled. 'Most people in Wales have got something to say about the Welsh language!'

'But you can't speak Welsh yourself, can you?'

There was a brief hesitation while he thought of an answer. 'Well not really. I can understand more than I can speak.'

'Why don't you learn?'

This time, the hesitation was even longer. 'It's difficult, living in London and all that, you know … ' The words petered out as he looked for another fig leaf. 'But I'm going to brush up a bit when I retire.'

For a few minutes, we talked about the growth in Welsh-medium schools and attitudes towards the language in places where it really was rarely heard in the streets, workplace or home. The Turk was keen to give me an example. 'Don't think you get too much Welsh around this part of the world. I've not come across it anyway.'

How well did he know Chepstow? Once again a careful, veiled expression came over his previously animated face.

'Not that well – a friend of mine moved here a year ago. Uh well, she's a Welsh speaker.'

'From Llanelli?'

With the same expression-free face he said, 'No, not really – a tiny village', he shook his head, 'you'd never have heard of it, miles from anywhere.'

'What does she think?'

'About what?'

'About local attitudes towards Welsh.'

'Some people couldn't care less about the language, others ... '

I broke in. 'But isn't that true of most parts of Wales?'

'Possibly, but it's probably more true in a place like this on the border – stands to reason – anyway a minority have got very, very strong views for and against the Welsh language and they're the ones who usually get heard.'

He smiled and told me a variation of something I had heard before. 'The other night, my friend asked me what's the correct term for someone who can only speak one language – she said there were two answers, but as she was generous, she would accept either one of them.'

'What did you say?'

'Monoglots.'

'That's right, isn't it?'

'Yes, I asked what the other word was and she said ... '

His build up was too slow, so I finished it for him. 'The English.'

'You knew it!'

This time it was my turn to smile. 'Don't think it just applies to them. Not sure too many Celts are multi-lingual.' He nodded grudging agreement before I told him he should follow a decent rugby team and left to talk to some locals in a town which had more hills than I ever remembered. The first problem was finding someone from Chepstow. I spoke to a likely looking couple and found they were staying in the area for the races. A few minutes later, I watched two young women sketching the famous Norman castle before finding out they had driven over from Bristol. Not that far away, I met a man, leaning against a wall that led to another supermarket. Unfortunately, my possible source of information could barely speak, let alone tell me about Chepstow, because he was suffering from one of the worst hangovers in the history of alcohol, but eventually I got lucky when I sat near two elderly ladies in a café. They were inquisitive, friendly and local! The place, although busy, was quiet enough to speak in without shouting and they were kind enough to answer my questions as best they could but one of them, the one with the silver-framed glasses, said, 'Don't expect too much!'

To begin with, they tried to help clear up a few mysteries I had come across when doing a little research for the trip – including the apparently thorny problem of addresses. I had looked at the website of a primary school in Sedbury, Gloucestershire and found that part of its postal address was given as Chepstow, Monmouthshire! Why? They did not really know, but one thought it was something to do with the way the post office or whatever it is called these days, organises its deliveries. A couple of days later I spoke to a man who confirmed it. He ran a Sedbury guesthouse and told me that of course it was in England, but for postal purposes, it had a Newport post code and was therefore in Wales – strange but true. A few like-minded people had tried to change things, but so far had not had any success. He was not a happy man and thinking about it, who can blame him? It comes to something when a postman can change your nationality just to make it easier to deliver junk mail.

After a few minutes, I asked the old ladies if they felt Welsh, British, 'border' or something else. At this stage, you might remember a rather earnest young woman on a bus to Hereford telling me she was a 'European.' Silver Glasses was again the first to answer the question. 'British, but I'm also Welsh.' Her slightly younger friend agreed with her. 'And me – we were brought up to be British, you can't change that.'

It was as if they had been rehearsing. It was the turn of the older woman to retake the lead. 'Don't *want* to change that, but it's all different now, isn't it?'

What did she mean?

'When we were young, things were settled – these days you don't know where you are.'

'Do you like living here?' They did, wouldn't live anywhere else, but they also said they wouldn't want to be walking around at night. Too rough. Too much noise. Too much trouble. Chepstow had changed.

'Is it a Welsh town?' They both thought it was. There was no question about it. It was in Wales so it was Welsh. I asked them what came to mind when I said the word 'England?'

'Not sure what you mean.' I explained and then for once, the first attempt to answer the question was made by the younger woman.

'I understand – well to me England is Gloucester, Bristol, London, those kinds of places ... ' She pointed down the road and said, 'It's just there, across the bridge, I don't think about it much – don't think many people do', before turning to her friend and appealing for support. 'Isn't that right?'

'Yes, probably. Right, my turn, England, let's see, cheese – Cheddar cheese, ham – Wiltshire ham ... ' She looked at me. 'I buy it every week, England's bigger than us, the Government's in London ... ' For a moment she hesitated before finishing with a bit of a flourish. 'Royal family, Buckingham palace and the Prime Minister!'

'Why have you put him in?'

'Because he's in London and London's in England.'

'Don't you think of him as your Prime Minister?'

She hesitated and then said, 'I suppose so, but I'm not sure these days – with the Assembly and everything.'

Using my own primitive visual aid, I pointed to the east. 'What do you think of English people?'

Silver Glasses was once again, the first to speak. 'Like us really. People are the same, aren't they?'

Her younger friend was not convinced. 'Well, don't know about that, don't think everyone's the same – if they were, we wouldn't be called different names, would we? They're called English and we're called Welsh – there must be a reason.'

I stayed silent, but the woman wearing the glasses nodded approvingly and said, 'You could be right. Hadn't thought of it like that.'

We finished the conversation with the topic of the moment; the furore that had erupted because some Members of Parliament milked the expenses system for every penny they could get. 'They claim for everything, and we only get our pensions!'

The older woman was working herself up. 'All those fiddles, it's disgraceful! I know what I'd like to do to them.' Her grim smile did not bode well for dodgy MPs if she was ever given supreme power.

What did they think of the Welsh Assembly? Not much. What about Assembly Members? Again not much, but some were not too bad. Were they glad Wales had some form of devolution? Not really. Were they proud to be Welsh? Both looked surprised to be asked – of course they were proud to be Welsh! I asked them why.

This time, it was the younger woman who was the first to speak.

'Because of the type of people we are, I suppose.'

Her friend did not take long to chip in, and then they were away at the races. 'Most people here are very nice – we try and help each other, don't we?'

'Yes, I think so and we've got all those actors … '

'And singers – Tom Jones'

'Bryn Terfel, Kathryn Jenkins, Charlotte Church … '

'And we're good at sport.'

'We won the rugby last year!'

I thought about my own mother and how she dealt with the stresses of watching a tense game when Wales were playing. As I was thinking of her wandering into the kitchen to make a cup of tea she did not really want, the women were about to finish with a flourish.

'We've got lovely countryside … '

'And beaches – we've got the lot!'

They both smiled with the pleasure of being Welsh. It was a good moment to smile back, thank them and get ready for the journey to England.

Sometimes on these trips you get lucky. The good-humoured retired couple waiting for the Beachley bus might have been sent by someone who had my best interests in mind. They enjoyed their weekly trips to places within a drive of an hour or so. It was Chepstow's turn today. He came from St Briarvels and turned out to be interested in all sorts of things, including accents and language. She was from Birmingham, but was at pains to tell me she had been born to Forest parents and that they both spend a lot of time 'helping people.' For the next few minutes, they helped me. As soon as I told them why I was in Chepstow, they were off and running.

Did I know that the Forest of Dean had its own dialect? Did I know some of the words seemed to be related to Welsh? I asked for an example. The man came up with the term used to tell someone to keep quiet.

'Not sure how you'd spell it, but once I saw it written down as 'highst' –

think that's right.' He spelt out the word letter by letter, before saying, 'Don't Welsh people use 'wysht' or something like that?'

'Yes, I say it myself. Any more?'

'Butty – friend, it's the same – the Yanks borrowed it for buddy.'

The American reference brought back memories of my father insisting that Elvis Presley's family came from west Wales. 'Originally it was Elfis Preseli, like the mountains – Elfis was Welsh alright.' I had smiled then, but had to put the thought away for now, because my Forest guides had moved on to ancient rights. And what wonderful words they used as they told me – sheep badgers, estovers, freeminers, verderers – the list went on and on, and I revelled in the power of the images that flooded my mind. I glanced at the pair and wondered why they were taking the bus.

'Don't really know.' Mrs Forester hesitated and then said. 'We thought we'd fill in an hour, never been there before, we're not getting off, are we?'

Her husband laughed, then spoke to me. 'No, retirement's wonderful – all this travel to exotic places. You've got all this excitement ahead of you!'

Did the people of the Forest have much in common with the Welsh?

'Don't know about that, not sure they do – not sure we've got much in common with anyone. We're a funny lot!' They were still smiling when our bus arrived.

Within minutes, we were crossing the bridge over the Wye on our way to Sedbury. I wanted to take a picture of the big sign that greeted us on the far side, but as is so often the case, I did not have a camera with me, yet as I did not own one, it was hardly surprising. Then I had an idea; I could use my mega something pixel mobile phone, but by the time I was ready to snap away, it was already too late. Pity, I would have liked a record of my first relevant bilingual sign on English soil: 'Welcome to England' – '*Croeso i Lloegr*', and wondered who had decided on the policy – Gloucestershire County Council, the Highways Agency, or a Welsh-speaking mole within the Civil Service. I was still thinking about the sign when the bus arrived in the village of Sedbury. A handful of us got off, but a few passengers and my Forester friends stayed on as it left for Beachley and the barracks that housed the 1st Bn, The Rifles. The temperature and humidity might have been rising in this part of the country, but they would be nothing when compared with some of the world's most troubled theatres of war where these soldiers, as part of the Commando Infantry Brigade, had served with such bravery and distinction.

In the village's newsagent shop, I spoke to a friendly, helpful young man and asked him which local paper was the best seller – the *South Wales Argus* or *The Forester*, which I assumed had something to do with a forest named Dean.

'*The Forester* sells a lot more.' It was as I had thought and in one sense, as it should be; after all we were in Gloucestershire, England, even if the Royal Mail thought otherwise. I asked about local accents. 'There's not much difference around here, but you always know if someone's from Wales – well somewhere in the valleys or places like that.'

'Could you tell if someone was from Chepstow?'

'No. Doubt if anyone could.'

There was a brief pause as he thought some more. 'On this side, the strongest accents start further in the forest.' He laughed and made a face. 'Funny lot, they use different words up there!'

I glanced at my newly reliable watch. It was time to make a start and so, in hot sunshine and under skies that could have come from a travel brochure, I left Sedbury on the last short leg of the journey. If you sense the man leaving the village behind was full of *joie de vivre*, then you would be wrong, because on a day as hot and humid as he had known since being in Brisbane, the man was beginning to have doubts. Why was he walking at all? Because this southern end of the long distance Offa's Dyke path does not have a handy bus stop, that is why. It was not surprising, given that the spot was surrounded by hills, marsh land, the River Severn, scrubby vegetation, small stands of trees, fences, styles and part of Offa's Dyke itself. But the man comforted himself with the thought it was unlikely to be too taxing – just an easy walk along a country road, followed by a stroll across what would probably be a few fields to his destination. We'll see ...

Within the first few hundred yards, my doubts had grown. Perhaps I should have got off the bus in Sedbury, looked around the village for a while, had something to eat and drink in the pub, then chatted to a few locals before getting back on a bus for the return to Chepstow – after all, as I kept telling myself, it was not as if I was writing a trail guide. But I had decided, for some perverse reason, that since I had seen the start of the path, I should make the simple effort to see it through. As the sun climbed even higher in a sky of faultless blue, I hoped that by the time I reached journey's end, that decision would be justified.

In less than a hundred yards, my shirt was clinging to me like a warm wet nappy worn by a frightened child. My rucksack, heavier than usual with accumulated rubbish, was beginning to cut into my shoulders. My eyes stung as sweat ran into them from hair that felt as if I had just come out of the shower. But in case you are wondering, my feet were fine, thanks. It was getting hotter. It was more like the Gobi than Gloucestershire. It was an exaggeration, but only just. I trudged on, reminding myself that in half an hour or so, I would have reached the southern end of the long distance footpath I had first seen on a freezing cold Prestatyn beach more than 150 miles away to the north and that this last gap effort, however pathetic it might seem to someone who had actually walked the whole length, would be well worthwhile. The thought kept me going for at least three or four minutes. Cars swept past me as I struggled up a little slope and looked for the Offa's Dyke path sign that should take me straight to my destination. I use the word should, but for reasons that would not shock anyone who knew me, I was not really sure, because I did not have an Ordnance Survey map or a proper guide which would take me step-by-step along the way. All I had was a little book which included less than helpful phrases like the walk starts and finishes near a plaque inscribed with the words *Llwybr Clawdd Offa* or Offa's Dyke Path. See what I mean? Occasionally, for variation, the author would include more descriptive, but still vague information, such as from time-to-time you get glimpses of the distant roofs of houses and banks of flowers – well thanks very much!

Just as I saw the wooden sign that meant I had reached the path, a motorcycle roared towards me ridden by a fit, strong young man wearing army fatigues and I was struck by the differences in our jobs. His would need guts and skills, mine only a bit of low-level perseverance. The first hundred yards of the path were a piece of cake. Birds sang in tune, insects buzzed around in the dappled sunlight and the leaves of hunched up trees and shrubs rustled in the warm breeze. A cheerful mixed group of men, women and excited children came towards me. The adults smiled, said hello and passed a few words as they shepherded their young flock. Judging by their accents, they were all Welsh. I asked the big man bringing up the rear if they had been to the end of the path.

'No, we've been sphering or zorbing or whatever they call it.' I must have looked puzzled, so he gave me more explanation.

'It's a big ball that they roll down the hill with people inside.'

Some television images came back to me. He pointed in the general direction of a hedge. 'Just over there, can't miss it.'

'Did you have a go yourself?'

He laughed. 'No, some of the children and the others did, but I'm not mad.'

'Where you from?'

'Pontypool.'

The happy man smiled at me and said 'Mind you, maybe I am, most people are around there. Enjoy your walk!' before hurrying off to catch up with the rest of the clan from Ponty. I watched and marvelled how anyone could move so quickly in this heat. The man from Pontypool was right; not far away behind the hedge, a sign on a small static caravan told me I was looking at the site of 'Chepstow Sphere Mania'. A few teenagers gathered around a giant, brightly-coloured inflatable beach ball, which shivered in gusts of invisible wind that travelled from the little valley below and left flickering grass behind in its wake. A tractor and trailer, presumably used for carrying the sphere back up the hill, waited to be called into action, but for the moment hung around waiting for something to do. For a few moments I stood watching, hoping to see something happen, but the only movement was the rise in temperature. To my right, a raised ridge curved down towards a little bridge; I had found a section of the dyke. I walked on and wondered what Offa would have made of it all. Would he have had a go himself? Would he have taken a cut of the profits? If there were two spheres available, would he have called the attraction 'Offa's Big Balls' or something similar? Only his wife could provide corroboration, but as she was not available, I continued down the steepening incline thinking it was unlikely we would ever know. With supreme mental strength, I put to the back of my mind the thought that soon I would be facing the return journey back up the hill from hell.

The narrow bridge had not been built over a proper stream, but a boggy stretch of ground. Once I had crossed it, I was faced with a difficult choice. Straight in front of me, the dyke climbed the other side of the valley. Slightly to my right, a muddy track headed in the general direction of some trees that masked the way ahead. I looked around for a signpost but could not see one. It was time to do some thinking.

I remembered a similar choice when I was accompanied by the estimable Comrade G. J. Morgan who, with his unfailing ability to express the extremely obvious had said, 'If it's bloody hot, choose the cooler path.' Following the dyke would be harder and hotter. There was no contest and so I squelched my way over marshy ground towards the shade of some trees, hoping I had made the right decision, but then, after a few minutes of bending under low-lying branches, sliding on brown, sticky mud and struggling past a dodgy gate, I found myself in open country. Perhaps fifty yards ahead, beyond the dark green of marshland, the broad, powerful river moved serenely towards its long term clinch with the sea. It was a quiet and hauntingly lovely scene that I knew would stay with me as long as I drew breath. Speaking of which, I had the momentary unwelcome thought that the return trek up that hill was getting ever closer. Light years away, silent traffic crossed the old Severn Bridge that linked two countries. The past came back to me – the ferry that once ran from Beachley to Aust on the Bristol side of the river, the picture of a young Bob Dylan waiting to cross for a concert in Cardiff, the opening of the bridge – it was all a long time ago when I still believed I could play for Wales or start a global empire.

The marshland turned out to be something else, or perhaps it had just dried out in the hot sunshine. Fronds of black seaweed lay on the ground within touching distance of the river. I got closer. The air was filled with the salt smell of sea in the middle of farmland – very strange, very nice, very alliterative – seaweed in Sedbury, but where was the end of the Offa's Dyke path? I did a 360° tour of my surroundings. Low cliffs, crowned by a compact mass of squat, sturdy trees began a hundred yards or so away to the north. In the middle distance, in front of those grey fissured cliffs, fifteen or twenty young people stood around as a taller, bulkier figure did a lot of pointing. I recalled the words of a couple of books I had glanced at in preparation for my journey – the path begins and ends at low cliffs. The bilingual plaque must be somewhere over there. Wherever it was, it was not worth the effort of finding it.

As my skin began to really feel the sun's prickly bite, I tried to memorise the view and think of something profound, but nothing came to mind. Should I wait until it did? But even I was not that dull. I took a couple of pictures on my mobile phone, then turned and set off back to Sedbury. Maybe inspiration would come later, but I was not going to hold my breath. The journey back started the way it had finished. The gate was still its awkward self, the mud was still muddy and low sweeping branches did their best to make things difficult, but I told myself that every single step of the way was taking me closer to a cold shower and an even colder drink. They had just finished loading the sphere onto the trailer when I crossed the little bridge and began to climb the slope hoping that a kind tractor driver would look across at a toiling man and offer him a lift, but he did not. There was no alternative but to walk on and up. At the top, I turned and pretended to look around me until my breathing returned to normal. The view was pleasant but would not detain most walkers for very long. Unfortunately, I did not have any real choice but to carry on. Before I reached the road to Sedbury, I met up with two young people who had just been sphering. Well he had, but she said she had more sense.

Did he enjoy it? 'Well, I'm not sure enjoy's the right word, it's different – bit the inside of my lip on the way down.'

'Would you do it again?'

'Maybe, don't know.'

His girlfriend (if that's what she was), smiled and said, 'I do. He wouldn't!'

They were from Risca, which was in Gwent before the latest round of local government reorganisation changed things in 1996. Even earlier, between the fifth and eleventh centuries, Gwent was a kingdom which for at least some of the period, had controlled this part of the Beachley peninsula. The road we had now reached was once in Wales. Just before we went our separate ways, the young woman pointed to my arm. 'You've cut yourself.'

I looked. Blood mingled with sweat and dripped down on land which poetic licence allowed me to call Welsh. I did some thinking. It must have been when I struggled past that gate. I mouthed an almost silent word – b******s! By the way, those who think the word is 'backless', are wrong. Why would anyone say backless? As they walked off towards their car, I headed for Sedbury leaving a crimson trail behind me. After a while, in an attempt to ignore the world outside my mind, and to pass the time until I reached the village, I went back to an old technique that was often surprisingly effective – trying to remember relevant quotations. Something about the heat perhaps? No, it would only make me feel worse. But what about distance? No, it would only make Sedbury seem further away than it was.

I glanced down at my forearm where scratches showed no sign of healing. But in all honesty, it was unlikely that these little wounds would figure in the *Guinness Book of Records*. Eventually, a Latin proverb, or more accurately, a gloomy Latin proverb came to me as indifferent drivers drove past – all the

hours wound you, the last one kills. For a second or so, a Celtic darkness descended on this sunny afternoon and I knew it was time to think of something more cheerful. Luckily a lovely play on words did not take long to arrive.

The words came from Pablo Picasso before he started feeling blue – 'When I was a child, my mother said to me "If you become a soldier, you'll be a general. If you become a monk, you'll end up as the pope." Instead I became a painter and wound up as Picasso.'

I smiled. I walked. I smiled again. The chemist would be open. The antiseptic would work. The sticking plaster would stick. The bus would arrive on time. It was getting cooler. The village was just yards ahead. I smiled. I walked. I smiled again.

A few weeks later

A FEW WEEKS AFTER the last leg of my journey, I sat down to write a final section which would be based on the profound conclusions I had reached about the attitudes and perceptions of those who live along the border between England and Wales. Twenty minutes later, not a single word had been written. It was all very difficult, perhaps because profound conclusions are usually the property of the intellectually or spiritually rich and even my mother would not claim I was either. Maybe I was being too hard on myself, because trying to reach general conclusions, however profound, that resulted from particular episodes or conversations, were always going to be problematical, mainly because most of them would come from the people I met en route. And people are complex beings. Widely varying vocabularies usually led to differing interpretations of the same question. Closed minds made it difficult to tease out interesting answers or conversations with people whose views sprang from crude national stereotypes did not help me make much progress. I could go on, but I think you get the idea. The problems did not end with the complexities of people, because my research techniques came from circumstances, opportunities and intuition rather than rigour and careful methodology. Had I even asked the right questions? Not always, but perhaps enough for the purposes of a book like this.

It was all very complicated, but border and broader issues are almost always complicated. It is not just far away countries like the two Koreas or India and Pakistan; places just around the corner have their own quarrels too, even if those quarrels are limited to name-calling or angry letters to the paper. Think of Lancashire against Yorkshire or battles to preserve the names and status of ancient counties and you might understand what I mean.

Had I found out anything by the time I had finished my ten trips? Yes, but nothing to excite the twenty-four hour news channels. And yet I had learned a lot. At the very least I had discovered that some of the beliefs I had held for years were based on the square root of bugger all. The journey also made me realise that some things which interested me – like the changing relationships between the countries of these islands, did not necessarily interest everyone I met in the towns I visited on the way.

Before I started, I wondered if the journey would give me the chance to meet people who held balanced views about the way Welsh and English people think about each other. It did. It also made me realise you do not have to go as far as Bleached Bones, Arizona, to meet eccentrics who would not recognise balanced views if they lived next door, let alone use them to help them frame their view of the world. And yet, and yet ... I began to suspect that even in the minds of balanced and moderate people, things were bubbling away. After all, most of us reach big conclusions based on lots and lots of little things.

Years ago, before stories about celebrity liposuction and the pre-nuptial agreements of actors who had once appeared on dog food adverts, filled the pages of countless glossy magazines; I used to work for British Rail. In an early 'orientation' lecture, a senior manager had told us that if a passenger saw a station porter with an egg-stained tie, the employee *was* British Rail. He had a point and years later it was the only point I remembered. Little things beget big thoughts.

An English family who endured a rainy bank holiday in Wales sometimes took it personally. A Welshman who had lost his childhood sweetheart to a multi-millionaire from London is someone who might want England to lose a World Cup qualifier against anyone. A Geordie who once tried and failed to buy a bottle of Newcastle Brown in a tiny Welsh hamlet is a man with bitter memories. Valley boys who remember that an English rugby referee once said 'the Welsh are like animals, sometimes you have to show them the whip', might not be too bothered if they hear that Sir Clive Woodward had lost his job. We are talking about little things, little illogical things that can sometimes shape the views of people from neighbouring countries.

But in the midst of all the weird and wonderful conversations I had on my journey, there were lots of thoughtful perceptive insights, not just into the feelings Welsh and English people had for each other, but the changing nature of contemporary Britain. I stared at the blinking cursor line on the blank screen. If profound conclusions were beyond me for now, perhaps it was time to adopt a less ambitious approach. Perhaps it was time to just write down any conclusions I had reached after a journey which had begun on the sandy beach at Prestatyn and ended on the muddy banks of the River Severn at Sedbury.

As I wondered where to start, I remembered some reassuring advice given to me in Whitchurch by a red-eyed gentleman of the road as they were once called, 'Don't worry too much about making generalisations – sometimes it's the only way to make sense of things.'

So on this basis, let the generalisations commence!

- As far as the United Kingdom is concerned, most young people think it is not. For them, history is past tense, what matters is the here and now, and now the countries on these islands seem to be drifting apart.
- Anyone over the age of sixty is more likely to say they feel British rather than those who are younger.
- There are people, who at a pinch, might be described as 'Border', because either their prime allegiance is to a town, village or some geographical feature like a valley, or more probably, because they do not really feel particularly English or Welsh.
- If sport is used as one measure of deep-seated feelings, it could be argued that at least some remnants of ancient enmities still exist under a patina of modern, civilised behaviour.

Other conclusions were even less profound, including the fact that there are probably more 'holistic eco-friendly sustainable wellness complementary bio-degradable therapists' in the Marches than anywhere else on the planet and that at any given time, in countless border homes, pubs and village halls, festivals are being organised in meetings chaired by people called Baz or Lizzie.

The border country appears to have more specialist museums or collections per square mile than most places on earth. You might not think museums devoted to cider, salt, silk, primitive Methodism, Nelson, Violette Szabo, Robert Owen, Dr Who, Myth and Fable etc are particularly specialised, but I suspect most people would.

Before my journey, I had no real appreciation of the vital role buses play in the lives of many people who live in small towns or little villages, and news that services, like the weekly trip that links Bishop's Castle to Newtown, are either under threat or scheduled for closure, made me fear for the most vulnerable members of rural communities.

Some conclusions were based on the changes in the way we use the English language. For instance, I soon realised that on both sides of Offa's Dyke, there has been an expotential growth in the number of people serving chips in a chip shop or beer in a pub who take your order and say 'That is not a problem'. Those who want to save time opt for 'Not a problem', leaving people like me slightly puzzled and wondering if I had missed something.

It did not take me long to realise that the timeless and unchanging nature of the countryside might be an urban myth. Change does not just happen in the big, bad cities.

Although legend has it that there are some people living in rural mid Wales, deepest Shropshire and darkest Herefordshire who still say 'railway station', only a fool would believe that all the change is bad. Some innovations, such as community websites which appear to offer a useful means of giving and receiving information, must be a good thing – at least for those who have access to a computer. But on the other hand, websites that casually pick up and carry Welsh towns and villages into England, have the power to irritate people like me. Examples of this can be found up and down the border – from a Flintshire hotel being placed in Cheshire to Hay-on-Wye being included in a list of Herefordshire tourist offices. The reverse is also happening, with places in England being included in websites which are meant to be confined to Wales, and although my primitive research suggests the practice is not on the same scale, it does not make it right does it?

Does any of this matter? I think it does and it matters whichever side of the border you live or whatever your nationality might be. Some of the local websites I looked at surprised me – especially those where such issues as the Welsh language, Welsh history, Welsh politics, Welsh economy, Welsh education were sometimes argued by individuals who offered nothing but vitriolic and often ill-thought out opinions. These people must spend many angst-ridden hours analysing the postings of those who held different views and then sending them messages larded with bile.

But it was also surprising to meet more English people than I had expected who actually live in Wales but go through their daily lives pretending they do not. For these people, the border does not exist – not because of some sort of 'We're all the same, borders are administrative conveniences, peace and love' kind of way, but because of other, more complex reasons. Some did not accept the concept of a Wales which had even an element of quasi-separate national identity – for these people, Wales seemed to be akin to a recently manufactured local government area such as Sedgemoor, Elmbridge or Central Bedfordshire. It was a kind of 'they'll rename it and reorganise it soon' mentality.

Others thought that while a village like Penyffordd might technically be in Wales, there was nothing at all wrong/strange/ incorrect in saying Penyffordd, Chester. Say no more, yet these people were often nice and polite and genuinely did not see why appellations such as the one given above would bother anyone.

The surprises were not just 'cross border' in nature. In parts of north Wales, for example, I met any number of people who seemed to have unexpectedly deep feelings of bitterness towards a Cardiff orientated 'Taffia' and a south Wales dominated Welsh Assembly Government. Speaking of which, most of the Welsh men and women I spoke to who had an opinion on the matter, thought that Assembly members were, in the main, intellectual and political pygmies.

But looking back on my journey, one of the biggest surprises was to find more people than I had suspected who appeared to have a subconscious (if that's the right word) belief, that Wales, large swathes of the Midlands and the whole of the north of England were created for the benefit of those who live within or near the M25. This belief leads to a 'please keep jobs and factory chimneys out of the national parks because we don't want to see anything but unspoiled countryside and coastline from our holiday home', way of looking at modern Britain.

Had I found any *real* differences between the people I had met since leaving Prestatyn – regardless of their nationality? Didn't everyone want essentially the same things, like a long and happy life, healthy wealthy children, security and peace in our time? Yes of course, but the journey still reinforced my general belief that Welsh and English people looked at the world and their place within it in slightly different ways. Give me an example. I can't, it's a bit like talent – hard to define, but you know it when you see it.

Just before finishing this book, I surprised myself by half keeping a promise. I might not have visited the Spaceguard Centre when I said I would, but at least I made it in the end. When I had first heard that just outside small, sleepy Knighton, some sort of facility was busy tracking asteroids and comets, I filed it away under 'New Age Hippie Astrology Love and Peace Centre.'

If someone was looking up at stars, it would be because they were lying on their back after too much hedgerow wine or using banned substances – you get the idea. But I was wrong. The views from the long and winding lane that leads up to the voluntary-funded centre reminded me once again how much of the border countryside is just that – countryside, filled with fields, forests, rough pasture, hills, river valleys, punctuated only by the occasional glimpse of solitary farm buildings or the cuddled up cottages found in tranquil villages. Sorry for stating the obvious, but I suspect many people who live their lives in built-up Britain would feel the same. As the minutes went by, the views got even better. It was if I was taking off in a very slow old aeroplane. Grass rippled in winds that brought trees to life. The narrow lane kept heading for the skies and soon I was on the shoulder of the highest hill looking across at rural Shropshire to the east and rural Wales everywhere else, with the defenceless land laying spread-eagled in front of me. I kept driving, wondering if I had missed the turning and thinking it cannot be long now. But there was still time for a couple of tractor-driving farmers to pass me as they went about their earthly business before I saw the sign which told me I had arrived at the Spaceguard Centre .

I parked the car and looked around. Within yards of the centre itself, I could see a mini version of one of those cowled buildings I had seen on the tops of Hawaiian Islands in one of those good for you Sunday-night television documentaries. They had housed telescopes and I guessed this one did too. A smiling woman stood in the open doorway of a neat and tidy brick bungalow, which seemed to be part of the little two-storey complex. 'Good morning, have you come for the tour?'

A few minutes later, I was being told about the potential problems of NEOs – Near Earth Objects – either asteroids or meteorites, which were heading our way. I had been told to ask questions whenever I wanted, and as I was the only visitor on this early Sunday morning, I asked away without worrying if I was taking someone else's turn. It turned out that the man who gave me the answers, was one of the driving forces behind the project. He was obviously knowledgeable, but did not hit you over the head with too many arcane theories or numbers which were not in context. I had always thought that space was for other people, but I found myself enjoying the visit. For the next hour or so, I learned a little more about stars, asteroids, meteorites, atmospheres, gases, minerals, temperatures, orbits, collisions, probabilities, gravity, theories, proofs, experiments, solar systems and time scales. I asked questions and tried to understand what had happened and what might happen, which theories were still standing and which had been demolished. Just after we left the small planetarium, my guide pointed in the general direction of Ludlow and told me that if an object one kilometre across, penetrated our atmosphere and collided with the earth, it would devastate an area the size of Shropshire.

While I tried to get to grips with his words, he added something to the effect that if the object was five kilometres across, we would all be in trouble. Something that big would start a chain of events which would make a nightmare seem like a pleasant little day-dream. I listened to the graphic description of meteor showers setting off massive fires, volcanic activity on a huge scale, tsunamis inundating low-lying coastal land everywhere, enormous damage to the ozone layer, the sun becoming obscured by the injection of dust and debris into the upper atmosphere, the consequent destruction of food chains and the almost unthinkable images of survivors blundering about in the darkness and bitter cold.

Were collisions on this scale likely? Yes, although we would have decades of warning. Could anything be done to prevent collisions? Yes, but it would need more international co–ordination and effort than we have seen so far. Just before the end of my tour, I heard about Project Drax – the attempt to find funding to install and operate a twenty-four-inch Schmidt camera which would allow a wide-field sky survey to detect Near Earth Objects and something of the problems encountered in meetings with officials from government departments. I thanked my hosts and walked out into the bright sunshine of a day in high summer.

For a few moments, I stood next to my car watching far away birds riding thermals and thought about my own journeys up, down and across the border, between two tiny countries on a tiny island on a tiny planet that was just one tiny pinprick of light in the unimaginable infinity of the blackness of our universe.

Had I learned anything that might conceivably matter in the grand scheme of things? Of course not, but driving back down that long and winding lane, my mind was filled with good memories of the times I had enjoyed since I had caught my first bus in Prestatyn, and while *On an Offa Bus* might not mean much to anyone else, it meant something to me. I had started with a title and ended with a book.